Not One World, but Two

A Miscellany of Preachments

To Darrisl,
with my best regards
from Ibeleur
Jorshui?

Feb 27, 2018, aur

LEARNED SOCIETY
OF THE JOHN PAUL II CATHOLIC UNIVERSITY OF LUBLIN

Publications of the Faculty of Theology
179

THE CHRISTIAN MORALITY IN AN ECUMENICAL CONTEXT SERIES

EDITED BY

SŁAWOMIR NOWOSAD

SINCE 1934

Vigo Auguste Demant

Not One World, but Two

A Miscellany of Preachments

Edited, with an Afterword, by
Sławomir Nowosad

Foreword by
Andrew Louth

Lublin
LEARNED SOCIETY OF KUL
JOHN PAUL II CATHOLIC UNIVERSITY OF LUBLIN

Reviewer
Prof. Paweł Bortkiewicz, SChr

Computer compilation and Index by
Stanisław Sarek

Cover design by
Marta and Zdzisław Kwiatkowski

Cover photo
Christ Church, Oxford, by Sławomir Nowosad

ISBN 978-83-7306-777-6
ISBN 978-83-8061-413-0

TOWARZYSTWO NAUKOWE
KATOLICKIEGO UNIWERSYTETU LUBELSKIEGO
JANA PAWŁA II

ul. F. Chopina 29/11, 20-023 Lublin
tel. +48 81 525 01 93, tel./fax + 48 81 524 31 77
e-mail: tnkul@tnkul.pl   www.tnkul.pl
Dział Marketingu i Kolportażu tel. + 48 81 524 51 71

Druk i oprawa: ELPIL, ul. Artyleryjska 11, 08-110 Siedlce

Contents

Foreword

FIRST met Canon Vigo Auguste Demant in the autumn of 1970. I had just arrived in Oxford as Fellow and Chaplain of Worcester College, Oxford, shortly to become a University Lecturer in Theology. Oxford I scarcely knew, having been a student at Cambridge and then Edinburgh. But I knew Demant's writings: he was something of a hero of mine, though my academic interests were to develop in the direction of patristics, not what Demant liked to call Christian Sociology. So I went to his house in Tom Quad in Christ Church and knocked on the door. I was wel-

Vigo Auguste Demant

comed warmly, if with some surprise. By the early 1970s, Demant had come to think that the world had passed him by and he was, I think, genuinely surprised that he was still read, and by someone so young (as I then was). That was the beginning of his last year as Regius Professor of Moral and Pastoral Theology at the University of Oxford, to which his canonry was attached. During that year, I visited him many times, often arriving for tea at about 4 p.m., and staying on for dinner in Christ Church in the evening, all the while talking (while he took snuff). In autumn 1971, Demant retired from his chair; he and his wife moved to a small cottage in Headington, a suburb of Oxford, where I continued to visit him frequently. Demant (he was always known as "Demant", even by his wife, at least when others were there) became one of the founding members of the Christendom Trust, set up around that time by his friend of many years, Maurice Reckitt, to continue to promote (mostly by supporting lectureships and research projects) the aims of the Christendom Movement, in which Reckitt and Demant had been the leading members. This theological movement within Anglicanism can be traced back to the years between the two World Wars.

It aimed to be orthodox in theology, but radical in its analysis of society. Demant was recruited by Reckitt as director of research, while continuing his vocation as a parish priest, and then from 1942 to 1949, Canon of St. Paul's Cathedral, London. Demant's energy and commitment gave the Christendom movement its intellectual coherence and even distinction. Its high point was perhaps the Malvern Conference, called by William Temple in 1941 (then Archbishop of York, shortly to become Archbishop of Canterbury) to discuss the role of the Church of England in the rebuilding of English society after the end of the Second World War. Temple's untimely death in 1944 dashed the hopes of that group. Something of the vision that inspired these men (they were mostly men, though one of the speakers at the Malvern Conference was Dorothy L. Sayers, the novelist and Christian apologist) can be seen, not only in the proceedings of the Malvern Conference (published in 1941), but in Demant's own books, such as *The Religious Prospect* (1939) and his Scott Holland lectures, *Religion and the Decline of Capitalism* (1952).

What was it that the Christendom Movement stood for? It was a form of Christian Socialism, though it embraced a somewhat idiosyncratic vision in which socialism meant, not some variety of Marxism or even liberal social democracy, as the nineteenth and twentieth century knew it, but harked back to more medieval ideas: "guild socialism", the idea that men (and women) found their identity and fulfilment in groups or communities, not defined by state or nation, but by beliefs and occupations. The "guilds" that characterized late medieval towns and cities and exercised power on behalf of their members, shielding them from the power of the emerging modern "state", provided a model for what Demant and others felt was necessary for a sane society. It is perhaps easier to identify what they were opposed to: individualism, a *laissez-faire* market system, which had led (as many had lamented since the eighteenth century) to the destruction of traditional communities, leaving individuals at the mercy of entrepreneurial market systems. But the Churches' response to this, indeed its very part in this development, these Christian socialists also deplored, for they saw the churches as responding, by and large, by moralizing: by preaching an individual morality that far from challenging the social structures that such individualism had created, simply took them for granted, and indeed often shored them up.

These Christian socialists believed that the Church should be mounting a critique of the social structures of modern society, attacking the individualism that lay at its root, and endorsing policies that would foster natural groups, such as the family and groups based on occupation and belief, to counter the unholy alliance between rampant individualism and a capitalist state. This was to involve an analysis of the structures of society, an analysis that would be informed by the Christian doctrine of what it is to be human, created in the image of God for communion with God and with other human beings. In this analysis they took their lead from the medieval theologians, especially St. Thomas Aquinas, and tended to view the society of the Middle Ages, "Christendom", through somewhat rosy spectacles. They were not alone in their enthusiasm for the society of the Middle Ages and its cultural achievements from gothic cathedrals to Dante: they were part of a movement of European thought that included scholars like Jacques Maritain, Étienne Gilson, Marie-Dominique Chenu, art historians like Émile Mâle, poets such as Paul Claudel and T.S. Eliot, and others, in England particularly people like Dorothy L. Sayers, Christopher Dawson, and Gilbert Keith Chesterton, who popularized an appeal to the Ages of Faith against a modern society that had lost both the Faith and structures for nurturing and fostering people rather than exploiting them. One aspect of their view of medieval society was of particular importance: the sense of a set of common values, informed by the Christian Faith, in terms of which people understood themselves, their lives and their actions. This notion of society as embodying values, in contrast to the more mechanistic ideas stemming from the Enlightenment, was central to those who thought in terms of "Christendom". T.S. Eliot's *The Idea of a Christian Society* expressed this approach with characteristic lucidity and passion.

Demant brought his Catholic, orthodox theological convictions to bear on the problems of interwar society. He wrote a number of works as (he put it) "an unorthodox economist and an orthodox theologian", analysing the seeming meltdown of Western civilization signalled by the inflation of the twenties, the General Strike, the Wall Street crash, and the depression of the thirties, together with the rise of communism, nazism and fascism, all of which sought to solve these problems by the exercise of totalitarian power in a way only open to a modern State, which fascism in particular justified by appeal to ideas very like those of the Christendom ideal. The first of these works was a report to the "Christian Social Council" of the Church of England "by its Research Committee", though, as Demant pointed out in preface, he alone was responsible for its arguments and judgments. It was called *This Unemployment: Disaster or Opportunity?* (1931). In it Demant went beyond the hand-wringing and palliatives such as soup kitchens, with which the Church had responded to the growing unemployment of the interwar period, necessary though such palliatives were in the immediate situation, and raised questions about the kind of society that had produced such employment: a society in which human beings were increasingly valued solely for their paid employment, but where the technological advances that had helped bring about this society required fewer workers. Such a society both reduced human beings to the status of worker (or employer) and at the same time required fewer people as workers: it was this contradiction that lay at the root of the real misery produced by unemployment, and made it impossible to see how the decline in demand for human energy made possible by technological advance might be regarded as an achievement and an opportunity. It was this contradiction that needed to be addressed. Demant warned against a mere palliative response, either by charity that did nothing to meet the insecurity and lack of value experienced by the unemployed, or by creating needs (not least by advertising) merely to increase the demand for labour. "A true order would be based upon the truth that consumption is logically prior to production, that it is more fundamentally true that we produce to live, than that we consume in order that we may produce and trade. To deny this order of priority would be to deny the value of all art, science and other cultural activities which have been made possible by the release of human energy from the necessity of economic activity". This was typical of Demant: to look beyond the immediate problem and ask questions about the values and structures of society that often, he maintained, concealed contradictions that produced the problems. As Reckitt used to say, "you can't moralize a contradiction"; and yet the Church's response to social problems was often no more than an attempt to do just that.

When I met Demant, he had been more than twenty years as an academic professor at Oxford, lecturing on moral theology and supervising research students. He was undoubtedly much valued, particularly by his research students. But in other ways he felt ill at ease. He was no scion of the Establishment: his father had been a member of the Comtean Church of Humanity in Newcastle; his mother, of Huguenot stock and Danish ancestry. He initially trained as an engineer, then as an anthropologist; before becoming an Anglican priest, he had ministered briefly as a Unitarian minister. Part of his schooling had been in France: he was essentially cosmopolitan. He once told me that, when he was engaged in the de-nazification process after the war (he spoke German, as well as French and Danish), he had been taken into the Soviet area of Berlin. His guide explained to him that she could not take anyone, certainly not the leader of the group Demant belonged to, the eminent Classicist, Sir Richard Livingstone (I think), who was altogether too obviously an English gentleman, but, Demant would chuckle, she could get by with an 'old cosmopolitan like me'.

On the desk in his study, both at Christ Church and in Headington, there were two photographs: of Nikolai Berdyaev (whom he had known in Paris presumably in the late twenties: he had attended, at least occasionally, the colloquy Berdyaev ran with Jacques Maritain), and of T.S. Eliot. He was, I think, uncomfortable at Christ Church, though devoted to the cathedral side of his duties. Once he acknowledged as much to me, saying that his real intellectual work had been essentially interdisciplinary (as we would say nowadays), alongside theology, he read economics, sociology, anthropology, philosophy, and in his writings combined all this; at Christ Church he felt intimidated with colleagues who were real economists, sociologists, and philosophers. Certainly his greatest works belong to the 30s and the 40s. In 1957–8 he gave the Gifford Lectures at the University of St Andrews in which he explored what he called the "natural history of Christianity", that is Christianity as a human activity in a social context. But these lectures were given *ex tempore*, and he never managed to publish the expected book of the lectures, although he did manage a brief article outlining their scope, which appeared in "Theology". I have seen and looked through the notebook in which he listed the themes of his lectures (on one side) and quotations he intended to use (on the facing side)—he appointed me his literary executor—and I remember thinking that, had this been published around 1960, as intended, the history of theology in the 1960s, at least in England, might have been very different.

As a priest, he preached frequently, belonging to a school that prepared sermons as literary pieces, carefully thought out and written down: these sermons were often preached on several occasions, and I recall the time when I persuaded him to preach at Sunday Evensong in Worcester College Chapel, hearing the crackling of the ancient leaves of paper as he turned from one page to another. He intended to publish a volume of these sermons, and prepared them for publication. It was to be called *Not One World, but Two: A Miscellany of Preachments*. He arranged it into six sections—Explorations, Doctrinal, General, Social, Commemorations, and a final section of obituaries (all of them, I think, sermons) of four people who had been of importance to him: William Temple, Michael Foster, T.S. Eliot, and Cuthbert Simpson—William Temple, the former Archbishop of Canterbury, who had been an early inspiration for Demant; Michael Foster, a philosopher who had been a colleague at Christ Church; T.S. Eliot, the poet, who had been a close friend of Demant's; and Cuthbert Simpson, who had been his colleague at Christ Church for most of his time there, first as Canon and Regius Professor of Hebrew (1954–9), and then as Dean of Christ Church (1959–69), also a close friend.

It is an enormous joy to welcome the final publication of this set of sermons as a tribute to Vigo Auguste Demant. I hope that their publication by Fr. Sławomir Nowosad and his forthcoming monograph on Demant will rescue his name and his thought from unjust neglect. It will be discovered that the problems in society he sought to analyse are still with us, and that his reflections on them as powerful as ever.

Andrew Louth

I. EXPLORATIONS

1. Knowledge and Goodness

"Be ye wise as serpents and as harmless as doves".
(Matthew x.16)

I

THIS IS MORE than a piece of advice; it is a precept or command of our Lord to His apostles. It sets forth the conditions for effectively carrying out the apostolic mission, which is to offer and secure acceptance of the gospel of salvation. We may take the words as meant not only to be heard by the priestly ministry of the Church, but also to be overheard by all Christians who have any responsibility for carrying the message to others, whether through specific teaching of the Christian Faith or through any secular education, which is informed by Christian conviction of the nature and end of human existence.

The command is given to the Christian messenger, who will put himself, by the nature of his character and his message, in as defenceless a position as that of lambs among wolves. If the Christian apostolate, clerical and lay, in England at this moment does not involve that kind of danger to its persons, yet the message itself and the Church, which enshrines it, are time and again in danger of being devoured by a number of causes, which seek to exploit the power of religion by asking it to sustain their own secular purposes.

But this call to the Christian apostle to embody that rare combination of the subtlety of the serpent and the simplicity of the single-mindedness of the dove, appears to be given unconditionally, we have to regret the mistranslation in both A. and R. Version, which gives in English "harmlessness" as the quality of the dove. Although this weakens the sense, it is not an altogether uninspired error, for we shall see that to refrain from doing harm requires in our sinful world the more positive virtue of sincerity, simplicity, all single-mindedness, conveyed by the original ἀκέραιοι [*akeraioi*] or the Latin *simplices*. There is not the same ambiguity with regard to the wisdom here associated with the serpent. It quite plainly means the prudence, subtlety, knowledge of the forces that move men, which we would call worldly wisdom. The command is therefore to hold together the qualities of worldly wisdom and singleness of mind or purity of heart; to combine knowledge and goodness.

To modern ears it seems as if the striking emphasis is to be laid upon the wisdom of the serpent as a mark of the Christian apostle; for we take for granted the simplicity of motive is the first fruit of his own conversion. And most people today would read it: do not only be sincere, cultivate also the astuteness of the serpent who knows where to get right into the vital centres of his victims or converts. It is likely, however, that spoken to members of the Jewish people who embodied some of the wily abilities of their forefather Jacob, this precept of Jesus may have put the stress upon the simplicity of the dove. In any case, it is a direct conjunction of qualities that is enjoined: Be wise *and* good; neither is a substitute for or secondary to the other. It is a direct rejection of the cynicism, which says: be strong, but if you cannot be strong, be clever: and if you can't be clever, be good. It is a call to be both aware of the nature of the world, to which the word of God is to be ministered and to be single-minded custodians and teachers of that word. In terms of our contemporary world situation, and in our modern jargon, it implies a condemnation of the utopianism, which ignores the relativities and mixed motives of the fallen world—and on the other hand the unprincipled opportunism that is concerned only for successful results.

In our attempt to discover what the Lord Jesus is saying to ask today in this word, we may find solid ground for encouragement in the fact that even our bewildered and largely apostate generation will naturally read "single-mindedness" as meaning single-mindedness in the pursuit of good. Unsophisticated men and women will not spontaneously recognise the possibility of single-minded devotion to evil. There is therefore something deep in the mind of us all, which detects the strength of simplicity in goodness and the weakness of complexity and inner conflict in the soul of those of evil influence.

But the difficulty of our modern situation is brought home to us when we have to recognise that it is easier to see the weaknesses that come from the separation of these two qualities of wisdom and goodness, than the strength and that comes from their combination, as we find it for instance in the great St. Bernard of Clairvaux.

II

I confess that the words of this text has haunted me ever since one evening in 1933 I read them in private in a village on the Rhine after the company, of which I was one, had listened with tense apprehension to one of the German Führer's earliest broadcast speeches as Reich Chancellor. There, I felt, is the wisdom of the serpent that knows just how to get into the springs of emotion and power in the souls of men, and to work outwards from there—converting next the intellect—and lastly compelling action in the desired direction. Here was no mere setting up of ideals and aims but the planting of seeds in the bed of men's souls. And I was led to consider the havoc wrought by such forces when opposed by the forces of goodwill that despise the wisdom of the serpent.

The most obvious weakness that has emerged from devotion to good causes without the wisdom that knows the world has been the belief of many Christians that in this sinful world the cause of right carries its own power. On the contrary, the Christian art of life consists in being ready to put power behind the right, with full awareness of the danger that power always brings terrible temptations to independence of moral responsibility. The danger must be faced and dealt with, and this can only be done by Faith in God who alone can keep power pure in us men. It is not only reluctance to use the arm of the state and of the sword that has deluded many Christians: there has also been a deceptive disposition to reject the power of the mind as something to put behind our moral and spiritual aims. Propaganda has got a bad name, in spite of the ecclesiastical origin of the term, and in spite of the truth that the New Testament itself is a propaganda pamphlet. And in so far as the Christian cause is in jeopardy today, it is largely because the Christian apostolate has shrunk from propaganda of that kind. We have squeamishly felt that it would demean our cause if we condescended to use the power of worldly wisdom in its furtherance.

Another example of goodness without wisdom has been the belief that we could meet an anti-Christian challenge, which relies on cultural and emotional transformation by means of ethical aims alone. English Christianity has been too much merely the custodian of moral ideals, it is ignored the need either to re-create a Christian culture in the outer framework of life, or to make real that inner culture of the soul that is the life of grace. Man is not strong and complete enough to practise the Christian virtues and to return to them again after he has fallen away, without a background to his goodwill, which carries him over the frequent patches when his will and perception are not at their best. That background has been provided in the history of Christendom by either or both the influences of a Christian civilisation and of experience of personal salvation in Christ, which stands when the more external supports of culture and civilisation fail. It is failure in wisdom to try to grow the plants of virtue and do nothing about the climate, in which they flourish.

Then, our modern Christian goodwill has not been wise about the nature of man himself. We have accepted the assumptions of the world about his nature when its good intentions have been manifest. Christian advice about world affairs has been stultified, for instance, by the notion taken from worldly idealism, that economic and commercial bonds between men were the deepest and most universal, political and national ones more restricted, and spiritual and cultural ones the most local and particular of all. And we have not seen that the defeat of all our best aims for world order has come from this turning upside down of the essential order inside human life itself.

That the most fatal result of lack of wisdom has been ignorance of the unruly, untamed forces in human life, which have been covered over by a haze of rational and ethical culture. The present uprush of these wild energies has reminded us with a shock that, after all, a Christian who has won some sort of real victory in his soul, should be something of an expert in satanism, and therefore wise before the historical event.

It is a long story this, of the frustration of good will for want of some of the wisdom of the serpent—and the story is no small part of the crisis of humanity and of the Christian community today.

III

But there is the other side; the story of how, in fact, so much knowledge has gone to seed—or been prostituted to base ends—for want of the simplicity or singleness of the dove, and how knowledge has failed of *wisdom* and degenerated into cleverness.

We have in our time realised something of where specialised learning with co-ordinating guidance was leading us. We have passed the stage, in which science made a fetish of details, with no power to serve the ends of life as a whole. But there is a considerable hangover from a period, in which applied science was a magician's bag of technicalities and in which each specialist was anxious to keep his domain separate from the others as if it were a property. Science is a great thing; but not all scientists are great men, and only a few are aware of the degraded position, in which the sciences have been placed by the civilisation they have done most to create; they have too often been suffered to exist as the flattered menials of democracy in its competitive or bureaucratic forms. This has induced a competitive outlook in the departments of knowledge, and a tendency in the scientist to claim primacy for this layer of reality, as a compensation for this sensed but unadmitted dependence upon the dominant social drift.

Science and Religion have at this moment a unique chance of burying an age-old hatchet, in meeting the threat of common exploitation by the wrangling contestants for social power. This is only possible on one condition: that teachers and practitioners of secular knowledge realise their need of a single-mindedness, which is beyond the power of devotion to a sectional interest to give; and that the prophets of religion take their part in and do not draw their skirts away from, the task of co-ordinating the disciplines that have given contemporary man such control over the means of living. This task will require such single-mindedness in the interest of man as will lead a number of teachers in both camps to make a sacrifice of the advantages of specialisation and be glad to become, out of sense of vocation, with the attendant loss of much that would be of personal value, good jacks of all trades. With the oncoming of the so-called planned society the danger will be great of the mere addition of sectional weaknesses and of conflict for place of control, owing to the all-too-human exclusiveness, jealousy and narrow ambition of the specialised workers, each set of which will be making a bid to persuade society that they have the vital principle of its health. Purveyors of knowledge, particularly in the scientific field, can no longer delude themselves or others with the theory that their sole function is to equip mankind with greater powers, entirely regardless of how these powers are likely to be used. That pretty theory, too obviously designed to console the learned and the apt for their painful subordination to stronger social forces, is not the expression of single-mindedness. The specialist in knowledge, if his unmixed devotion to his subject means no concern for the use that men as they are will make of his contribution, may be a single-minded scientist but he is a double-minded man. For when he buys a collar-stud in the market place or quarrels and makes it up with his wife or adopts a political attitude, he has a stake in situations, in which the consequences of his knowledge may be involved, and he has to handle those situations as a man who happens to be a scientist and not as a pedant who happens to be a man.

In brief, our equipment for knowledge and control of material, whether physical or human, can become a boon to man only if its experts see their activity as a part of their own life as whole *individuals*, to use that term "individual" in the sense of that, which is indivisible, rather than in its unfortunate derivative sense as that, which is divided from others. To be "the individual" is to be single-minded, and "the individual", as Søren Kierkegaard and his philosophical followers are continually reminding us, is a religious product. It comes not from the human attempt to unify our interests and experiences, for the perennial vanity of the soul cannot prevent *expertise* taking possession of the whole man; it comes from response to the unfathomable calling of God to be *this man* and no other, with all his faculties drawn together because their personal centre is recognised as given before its separate activities start going their own way.

But not only is recovery of wholeness or simplicity by the divine call necessary to save the world from disintegrated knowledge, which does not by itself serve wisdom; it is also impossible to know to whom we are speaking when we offer the Christian Gospel, without our own conversion to single-minded goodness. It did not take Karl Marx or Friedrich Nietzsche or Karl Mannheim to convince the Christian man who knows his need of redemption, that there is a human and interested bias in all our knowing. We see others, as persons or groups or nations, in relation to *our* needs. What they mean to us colours our picture of what they are. We know them not as themselves, which is as God sees them, but through grasping or defensive spectacles. We attribute a full measure of freedom to their behaviour, while we are conscious of the determining circumstances in our own. The terrible deadlocks of human history, breaking up in violent conflict, can all be traced to this bias in human understanding, which expects the other party to relieve the tension from his end. As the old jingle has it:

> "Lord Chatham with his sabre drawn
> Was waiting for Sir Richard Strahan;
> Sir Richard longing to be at 'em
> Was waiting for the Earl of Chatham".

That is the nature of humanity's tragic predicament. Each waits for the other; and my knowledge of the other is concerned with whether he furthers my purposes. It means that our true knowledge of others depends upon disinfection from the bias, which regards them as means for solving our own problems. That bias is only eliminated in proportion as we become *freed* from dependence on them for our own value and significance, and that is when we find it in God instead of in the world. There was a man in English journalism who passed to his rest a year or two ago, who got more out of his younger contemporaries than any of his colleagues. The secret was that he wanted nothing; spiritually he had found his meaning; both his encouragement and his criticism where entirely fruitful of creative growth in those who sought contact with him. A faint replica of God's dealing with man; because He needs nothing of man He knows what is in man without *arrière pensée*, just the plain truth.

Here we see the deepest link between wisdom and true goodness. Knowledge of the human forces the Christian messenger has to deal with is given to those only who can look without wanting—who have achieved some measure of single-mindedness, which can ask what other men need for their healing instead of what they can be made to do for ours. Knowledge of other men cannot be single-minded unless it is underpinned by the supernatural charity, which alone is free from dependence upon *their* coming up to scratch. For God alone gives to us His own power to love men before they are lovable; that is so that they may become so. Salvation gives the freedom, in which we can take the initiative in breaking the deadlocks of human relationships, because in Christ the redeemed man knows that the forces, which move from within, are stronger than those, which move in upon him from outside. His fears of what men may do to him are cast out by the love, which has strength to spare, because it is not all used up in concern for one's own existence and recognition. Membership in Christ means that the roots of our being are in the eternal world beyond the relativities of our human politics. And this freedom, which is another name for charity, is indispensable for knowledge; for with our inordinate egoism of soul we cannot be fair unless we are more than fair, that is unless we are generous. So the wisdom, which genuinely seeks to know the truth about the human situation, for the proper apostolic strategy, requires the simplicity and singleness, which is the fruit of salvation.

The two qualities laid down in the dominical precept turn out to be two sides of the same life in God, and as in the case of many such frequently contrasted qualities, their contrast and apparent incompatibility in this world appears to be one of the consequences of the disorder of human existence, which Christians call original sin. That is why, when men try to reconcile or identify them too cheaply, somewhere short of radical despair and its cure by faith and hope in the living God, then the most subtle deceptions arise. When this conjunction of wisdom and goodness, given as a divine imperative, is taken to be a theory, which would explain one in terms of the other anywhere short of the redeemed life, then we are being tempted of the devil. Is goodness only another name for knowledge? Is it true that *tout savoir est tout pardonner*? Just sufficiently near the truth to become the most dangerous heresy, for evil ever resides in the will and not in the intelligence. The danger is great today, when many men of goodwill, whose special province is a ministry of the understanding, are so anxious to heal the wounds of humanity by knowledge of historic causes or of psychiatric disorders that they often tend towards a debilitating neutrality in face of the stark moral challenge.

At this crucial moment in the history of Christendom, the two qualities of ability and goodness seem to be divorced beyond recall, and in some aspects are really in opposed camps. At such a moment it is a sure ground of hope to be reminded that their unity is not a consummation to be torturingly manufactured at the end of the human quest, but in fact underlies the beginning of it; and that their opposition is not in the nature of things but part of the moral struggle, which would never have arisen unless the two were originally one. Their actual contrast need not discourage us when it is seen as the result of man confusing, during his pilgrimage *in via*, the counterfeit and removable baggage of his self-will with his inalienable carriage of the image of God in the centre of his being.

2. Questions and Answers

"The whole multitude of the country of the Gadarenes
round about besought Him to depart from them;
for they were taken with great fear".
(Luke viii.37)

TWICE in the New Testament it is recorded that someone told Christ to go away. In one case, St. Peter, after the miraculous draught of fishes, calls out "Depart from me, for I am a sinful man, O Lord"; in the other, Christ had delivered a man from possession by evil spirits, which he caused to enter into a herd of swine who then drowned themselves in the lake: and the inhabitants then begged Christ to go away. If anyone thinks that the men of Gadara asked our Lord to go away because He had destroyed their pigs, that person shows that he understands neither human nature nor the Gospel, which is given for its healing. To imagine that these Palestinian peasants were filled with fear out of concern for their property is to apply to all men, at all times, what is applicable to a great deal of modern life—an economic interpretation of human facts.

I

It is a strange ending to the story of a great deliverance. Jesus had come across the water, and found there a small community, harassed and troubled by a poor, demented creature filled with evil spirits. He was so wild and fierce that, as we are told in St. Mark's version of the story, they could neither bind him nor tame him. Christ came, and at one stroke took away the terror, in which probably travellers had gone when they had to cross the mountains and pass the tombs, in which he dwelt, the terror, which must have scared the children when the man possessed had made an inroad into the town. And one would expect that, when they were delivered from that scourge, their main feeling would be one of gratitude and welcome to Him Who had delivered them.

But no. They all with one consent besought Him to depart from them; for they were taken with great fear. What was that fear? It may well have been the fearful awe at the presence of unearthly spiritual power, able to overcome more familiar force: it may have been embarrassment at the nearness of overpowering holiness—but the brief context suggests that it was rather the fear that is in all of us when we are faced with the prospect of being delivered from the problems, to which we are accustomed and required to face new ones. This demoniac had been a terror, a menace to his neighbours; but at any rate, he was their own, a kind of domestic danger, even a village character. And most of us can put up with a great deal if it is our own, something near and familiar. As Touchstone said of Audrey in *As You Like It*: "An ill-favoured thing, sir, but mine own". We can imagine these people of Gadara building up their existence round the unfortunate man in their midst. He had become a popular topic of conversation, the subject of village gossip. They had become interested in, and accustomed to, his habits. Possibly they had learned just how to avoid the times and places, in which they stood in greatest danger from him. He was a familiar problem, an accustomed difficulty. Now comes a Stranger, and takes it right away, not helping them to deal with it on their own lines, but removing it entirely from their lives. Someone Who comes, not asking them: "What are your difficulties, and how can I help you"; but removing the problem that had occupied a whole community, and thereby driving them back upon other and more important matters.

That is what human nature does not like, and it is exactly what happens when God enters a man's life. He does not give you an answer to the questions that you have been bothering about, perhaps for years. What He does is to take them away, and set you a new question altogether. Very often our human nature and the vanity of our soul make the very problems and difficulties, about which we groan, a source of secret satisfaction to us. So long as they are our own, of our own handling, we rather like them, even though sometimes we curse them. The point of this incident in the Gospel is that, when God comes to man, He changes the question that man has to ask and answer. He brings not a better answer to the same question, but a new question, a new problem, and a new task.

II

Take three simple examples of the way, in which, if you have accepted God in your midst, your questions will be different. One from Christian doctrine. Men often ask about the truth of our belief that Jesus Christ is Almighty God, and they put the question in this form: "How can a man be God?" In that form the question has no answer. But if you face the living God in your own life, you will learn to turn that question round, and ask, as the great English theologian of the eleventh century, St. Anselm, asked in a famous book, not why or how can man be God, but why did God become Man?

Or take the problem of ordinary human life and personal relations. We commonly ask of another, whether he is a likeable or lovable person, in order that we may decide whether we shall love him or not. If you put the problem of your fellow man in that fashion, you will never answer it. But if you put the question as God puts it you will ask, not is he a lovable person, but how may I love him in order that he may become lovable? Learn to turn your questions round. Put away the problems that bother you. Try to see things as God bids you see them.

Or take another example from the public life of the present day. There is great fear of war and catastrophe, perhaps the ruin of the edifice of our civilization. How, it is asked, can we stop war? But if we had the courage to put the question another way, and ask: what makes us dissatisfied with this or that kind of peace? we should immediately be confronted with a revolution in the whole of our organised way of life. If the world were summarily delivered from the threatened scourge of war, it might well, in its present condition, be as much bewildered and fearful, as were those men of Gadara, when confronted with an abrupt change in their habits of life and in a chief topic of opinion.

It is a mistake to think, as many people do, that men are guided chiefly by love of ease or gain. There is an incident in a book by Mr. Hilaire Belloc, in which he describes a walking tour he once made in the South of France. One day he came across a dealer in wines who haggled strenuously over the price of what he had to sell. But a day or two after he gave away, when met again, his wine for nothing. It only shows, says the writer, that what men most want in this world is neither gain nor comfort nor riches, but their own way. We will often put up with a great deal of trouble and inconvenience, and make ourselves and our fellows miserable, in order to get our own way, and our own way—to which we cling tenaciously—is not always for the pleasant things; often it is for our accustomed methods in shouldering our burdens or grumbling about them. We get a kind of spiritual vested interest in our difficulties.

III

It is my privilege sometimes to help people who come to me with their personal problems. It often happens that I have detected that what is really bothering them, the root of the matter, is not, as they imagine, some difficulty in the office or in their sphere of work. This is only a camouflage, a disguise, hiding a deeper problem that lies perhaps in the domestic sphere. When I point this out, the person concerned is often apt to be resentful at the notion that his problems are other than he imagined. But sometimes he will come back and say: "You were right, after all. I find that life is more manageable now that I see my problem where it really is".

If you struggle with difficulties or problems time after time without success, you can be assured that you are stating them in the wrong way. You are really evading the questions, which God is presenting to you, refusing to accept the problems, which He would have you solve, and are clinging to the questions and problems of your own. You are showing that lack of faith, which springs from the great vanity of the human soul. If you are sufficiently believing to accept God's questions rather than your own, you will find that a spiritual revolution has been wrought in you.

When organized public life is built upon that lack of faith, which clings to old problems because we have been accustomed to handle them in a particular way, there arises a state of crisis or deadlock. Many observers tell us what is the matter with our modern social life, but neither their diagnosis nor their remedy brings about an improvement.

It may help us to see what is wrong if, by an exercise of fancy, we transport that peasant community of Gadara into our twentieth century civilization. Cannot you see them dealing, in terms of modern organization, with all the problems created by the demoniac who lived in the mountains and terrified his neighbours? Police patrols ordered to ensure that those who travelled in his vicinity would go in safety; perhaps a special by-pass would be constructed in order to avoid him altogether. A welcome revival of industry would come from the manufacture of weapons of defence against the poor unfortunate lunatic. A vast trade in medicines would grow up. There would be advertisements and campaigns to counteract the spread of the dread disease, which afflicted him. Societies would be founded to bring pressure on the government for his extermination. Other societies would arise for his protection. City councils would be divided for and against. In a word, a vast human organization would be built up in order to deal with the evil. Can you not see what a calamity it would be if the evil were suddenly removed? It would mean a revolution. And this is precisely what happens when God comes into our life, and requires us to look at our problems as He sees them, not as we have been accustomed to handle them. We are confronted with a challenge of faith.

I am convinced that one of the great problems of modern life, about which we have been worrying for years—the problem of unemployment—has been wrongly stated from the start. As we have tackled it, the problem has been one of how to find work for the workless. If we had listened to the voice of God, our problem would rather have been how to use the bounty, which He bestows, how to make available the good things of life with just the amount of work required for that end. Had we put the problem in that form, we might have had an answer long before now. As it is, by stating it in our old accustomed way we seem as far as ever from its solution.

IV

The same obstinacy to go our own way has unhappy results in our personal life. Our everlasting busi-ness, our preoccupation with problems of our making, are so many excuses for our human failings and vanities. Sometimes our work becomes an alibi, like the man in the front row at a revivalist meeting who was asked by the missioner: "Are *you* saved?" He replied: "Oh, I don't have to be, I'm a reporter". Our preoccupations give us an easy conscience in avoiding the truth about our real selves; they provide suitable occasions for those sacrifices, about which we love to brag. They help to account for, or to cover, our failings in ordinary human relations. Once we rid ourselves of them, we should have to face our wives, our husbands, our brethren and our friends, as human beings. We should have to face our own souls and come to terms with God. But we are afraid of doing this, and we bid God depart from our coast. When God comes into a man's life, as He came to the town of Gadara, He bids him give up his own problems, and accept others. When St. Paul talked of repentance, he used a word, which means something much more than a mere emotion of sorrow for past misdoings. It involves a complete change of mind, a readiness to see all things in a different light.

The Bible from beginning to end is not the story of man's problems about God, but of God's problems about man. It is not an account of man's attempt to solve his problems with the Lord to help him, but of the way in which God finally sets the human problem in His own terms. You must have noticed that our Lord Himself hardly ever answered a question with a plain answer; it was His practice rather to put another question. He bids us find out how to do His will in His way. That is the hardest kind of choice that we are called upon to make in this world, harder than to choose good instead of evil. If we are to give up our own way of doing good, and find what is God's way in the particular situation, in which we are placed, to learn what are the problems that God sets us and accept them in place of our own, it is not enough to be interested in religion, it is not enough to learn and read about it. We must surrender ourselves to Him in worship and in prayer. We must learn to understand the meaning of God's own words about Himself in the Bible and in the Creeds of the Church, in the forms of worship that are given to us and in the prayers, by which we seek to discern His will. If we are ready to face the question that God asks about us, we make an act of faith because we know that, as it is He Who sets the question, and not we ourselves, He will also provide the answer.

3. The Spiritual Arena of the Moral Struggle

"Every Kingdom divided against itself is brought to desolation;
and a house divided against a house falleth.
And if Satan also is divided against himself, how shall his kingdom stand?"
(Luke xi.17)

THE LAST JUDGMENT means two things. One, that there is a real and objective distinction between good and evil, even though that distinction is so blurred in history to us who are involved in it; even though our estimates are often so mistaken that at the final assize those we thought first will be last, and the last first. Still the distinction and contrast between good and evil is an ultimate fact, which it is Christ's work to disclose.

And, in the second place, this absolute character is not to be revealed until the last time, at the end and fulfilment of history. Only in that judgment, which is the *last* judgment, will the separation and contrast between the good and the evil be manifested in unambiguous clarity. We may not, then, while we are *in via*, nor may our successors in some undated millennium, identify any of the positions we take up in the moral struggle with the place of judgment, which Christ holds at the right hand of the Father. In brief, good and evil are so intertwined in the actions of men, and in their collective behaviour, that the Wheat and the Weeds cannot be and will not be separated except by the divine harvester at the last day.

And yet, we have to live and to act and to judge, while in our historical situation, however sensitive we may be to the truth that "no man living is justified". We have to act as if that objective contrast between good and evil is not only an eschatological fulfilment, but also a present operative criterion.

The perennial urge to make our judgment of peoples, of causes and movements, mirrors of the absolute judgment of God, because we have so desperately to act with all our energy, is fortified when the causes are mixed up with almighty ideologies that draw religious forces of the soul with their services. When, in fact, the ineradicable demand of the human heart for a last judgment falsely seeks its fulfilment in some temporary achievement of social cohesion, which its devotees really equate with the final overthrow of evil in history, at least in principle.

It is a terrible and significant mark of our period that men seem incapable of acting whole-heartedly in the struggles of their time without the fantasy that their judgments have the absolute character of the last judgment. And this in a period when the intellectual guides are loudly insisting that traditional moral judgments have no central or normative force—but are relative and shifting, and merely ideas serviceable to a particular sect in the general flux.

It lays a heavy task upon the Christian mind to minister to the human problems in this situation, the task, namely, of giving religious backing to the reality of moral distinctions within the mixed good and evil of all human endeavour, which is all that history in the concrete offers. And, at the same time, to disinfect every world-perfecting endeavour from the pretensions that it carries backward into the present the final absolute character, which belongs only to the judgment of Christ at the last day. It is a task that has been made the more daunting—and the more necessary—in that Christian thought has largely lost sight of the Biblical and theological setting of the moral arena.

We cannot recover that setting by a few neat ethical formulations. That is possible only by looking again and again at one and then another aspect of that setting—so that we begin to live in the spiritual scenery, as it were, which was habitual to those who have learnt Faith while wrestling with the moral problem.

Here is one aspect of the setting, in which Jesus did place the conflict of good and evil during His ministry on earth. It will not illuminate the whole matter from question to answer, but it will take us a little way towards recapturing the specifically Christian context of the drama of good and evil in conflict. "Every Kingdom divided against itself is brought to desolation and a house divided against a house falleth". It is our Lord's answer to those who had accused Him of being in league with the devil, because He had cast out an evil spirit from a suffering man. "By Beelzebub, the prince of the devils, he casteth out devils".

The answer in effect says: if this were true, if it is by one demon that I cast out another, then the realm of evil would be divided. Christ calls that realm a Kingdom; He also calls it a house, taking up the metaphor conveyed by the name "Beelzebub", of which one probable meaning is "the Lord of the Mansion". "If Satan also is divided against himself, how shall his Kingdom stand because ye say that I cast out devils by Beelzebub".

The answer takes for granted a premise the hearers were supposed to accept. It is as if Christ said: "You know that the Kingdom of evil *does* stand; you know it is very powerful, you know it is united, that it will not fall down by its own inner divisions at the first puff of virtuous breath. Therefore this idea that Satan is in me and in the spirit I oppose, falls to the ground".

The picture is of a realm of evil—not a string of isolated evil acts—but a closely knit realm—Hell being perhaps the model state so far as organisation is concerned, besides which all human planning is amateurish and feeble—a force, which invades the human house and takes possession of it. This picture is in sharp contrast to that of our usual pelagianised scheme, in which the soul is supposed to be a unity, turning this way or that, with a united front—and able to assume that when it faces evil it is confronted with an army already stricken with division. On the contrary, we are here advised to recognize that it is the house of man that is divided and that the realm of evil is its superior in cohesion and efficiency. Even this delineation would be a salutary help if it stood alone. But, of course, it does not.

There is in this same Gospel perspective the announcement of another force—which is the sole superior in power to the Kingdom of evil. And it is as far from a collection of well meaning acts of human goodness as the realm of evil is from a sense of evil acts and wills in men. *This* is the Kingdom of God described by St. Paul in precisely this same idiom of realm. He writes of "The Father who delivered us out of the power of darkness and translated us into the Kingdom of the Son of His love" (Colossians i.13). Salvation is a counter-invasion. And we have our Lord's own warrant for this account of the situation. "When the strong man armed keepeth his court his goods are in peace, but when a stronger than he shall come upon him and overcome him, he taketh away from his whole armour wherein he trusted and divided his spoils". And the identity of the stronger man is made plain by the preceding sentence, which makes the link between the argument of our text and this parable of the two powers contending for possession of the house. "If I by the finger of God cast out devils, then is the Kingdom of God come upon you".

Here then is a New Testament presentation of the spiritual setting of the moral problem. It drives home its lesson by leaving out for the moment the will and intuition and talents of the human being, who is here represented as a kind of empty structure without a proper tenant. We have to look elsewhere for the counter-balancing truth of man's responsibility. It is not hard to find, but never quite cut away from this context of rival spiritual powers. Christ says to the Pharisees on the eve of His arrest: "This is your hour and the power of darkness" (Luke xxii.53), putting together the truth that men's acts are really their own and that they are at the same time taken hold of by outside forces.

We may change the metaphor to a more modern one in order to see that this picture of opposing spiritual forces surrounding man in a struggle for possession does not deprive him of responsibility for the outcome. Our bodies are open to the health-giving power of food, sun and air and to the disease germs, which are always in and about our tissues. This does not negate our power to determine, which of the two influences gains ascendancy in the blood stream. In both cases it is a long-term responsibility and cannot be exercised by a bare act of the will in the moment of crisis. I cannot by an act of decision settle whether I wake up in the morning with or without a bad cold. But the way I have lived over the past fortnight, in the matter of exercise, diet and frame of mind, may well determine the outcome.

How then does this configuration of the moral struggle help us to get in right perspective the valid but ambiguous moral judgments men have to make in actual life and their relation to the last judgment of Christ, which alone is an absolute discrimination of good and evil? I warned you that we should only be helped a little way. Even so, we may conclude by asking what, then, is the object, which Christ judges. His judgment is certainly a judgment upon persons, not upon acts, or intentions or results. But where are we to look for the quality in persons, which is the criterion of God's final assessment. We do not need the Christian Revelation to show us the mixture of good and evil in every human existence, personal and collective. On little illuminated cards in some houses we visit we sometimes receive the reminder that "there is so much good in the worst of us, and so much bad in the best of us—that it ill behoves the rest of us"—and so on. But, less sentimentally than that, we have plenty on hand in the sphere of politics, which is concerned with the problem how precisely good and evil are mixed in our own society, or in social systems with a total claim to moral finality, our own and its competitors. One insight to be got from this New Testament presentation warns us that the way good and evil are joined is not by some kind of numerical addition, side by side, as it were, so that one might be eliminated and the other left. Moral judgment cannot be made in quantitative terms, so much good, so much bad, but only in terms of the way one set of forces invades the house and disarms, or uses the other.

The power of evil to use the best impulses and talents of men is obvious enough. In order to deceive others our lie had better be mixed with a large element of truth; arsenic will be the more potent for poisoning your father if dissolved in a good wholesome beverage; there is loyalty among thieves; the worst tyrannies are tyrannies of the good. The way evil fastens on the good we know a great deal about, and it gives the moral problem of man its character as a tragic drama.

Do we know anything of the inverse process, that, in which the good fastens on the evil and turns it into an instrument of healing and salvation? We do, but it is not a piece of natural knowledge. That process is the working of the Kingdom of God and of Him who is the bringer of the Kingdom. I know of no better recent statement of this than in words of Charles Williams, for whom the battle of the kingdoms was a favourite theme:

"The Thing that was Christ Jesus, knew all things in the deprivation of all goodness... The Passion and the Resurrection have been necessarily divided in ritual and we think of them as separate events. So certainly they were, and yet not as separate as all that. They are two operations in one; they are the hour of the coming of the Kingdom. A new knowledge arises. Men had determined to know good as evil; there would be but one perfect remedy for that—to know the evil of the past itself as good... The Adam and their children had been involved in a state of contradiction within themselves. How could the simple knowledge be restored?... The thing has happened, the Kingdom is here... All is most well; evil is "pardoned"—it is known after another manner, in an interchange of love, as a means of love, therefore as a means of the good... [Pardon] is the name now given to the heavenly knowledge of the evil on earth; evil is known as an occasion of good, that is, of love. It has always been so known on the side of heaven, but now it can be known on the side of earth also". (*He Came Down from Heaven*, pp. 58 f.)

That is a profound hint. To know the evil of the past as the occasion of good is the prerogative of God and this is the mystery of it. But those who have in their own life appropriated that unclaimable and unmerited gift with regard to their own evil, can in some delegated way be vehicles of its transfer to other's evil.

As the evil has fastened on the good, so now the good fastens on and uses the evil of the past. As Joseph said to his brethren: "Be not grieved or angry with yourselves, that ye sold me hither, for God did send me before you to preserve life..." (Genesis xlv.5).

The moral drama of humanity in its full depth cannot be set in a context of moral idealism, of values, aims, intentions and will; but only in that of a spiritual cosmos, in which the stronger man armed—Christus Victor—takes away from the usurper what he is always stealing from God and he steals the God in us. But man has a real power to open and shut doors on both sides of the house.

II. DOCTRINAL

4. Maker of Heaven and Earth

"In Him all things consist".
(Colossians i.17)

ANNUALLY the Church calls our attention to the doctrine of God as Creator, and does this on Septuagesima Sunday, seventy days before Easter, which proclaims a kind of new creation. And we repeatedly recite a creed, which begins: "I believe in God, the Father Almighty, Maker of Heaven end Earth". All the clauses, which follow, including "the Life everlasting" are statements declaring what "I believe in God" means for a Christian. I need not remind you that the Apostles Creed is a document of the Church, containing the skeleton of belief implied in the Gospel, which the Apostles preached. You can get a good idea of what that message is if you read the sermons of St. Peter and St. Paul in the Acts of the Apostles, or then study its message in the First Epistle of St. Peter, with perhaps the help of Professor C.H. Dodd's *The Apostolic Preaching*. These accounts all say one thing, namely that in the happenings connected with Jesus who is called Christ, God had started a new history inside the old. Salvation, the new life, is the work of the same God who created the World. The first Christians had a tremendous sense of being part of a new creation, and we might say that Christian theology began with thought about how the Saviour, who inaugurated a new creation could be the same He who made the original creation. So while we declare our stake in God as creator in the first clause of the Apostles Creed; the idea of God, the creator, came second in the experience of the Church.

It is worth considering what we are doing when we affirm our faith by statements beginning "I believe in", for example in God the Father almighty, in the Forgiveness of Sins, and so on. To declare: "I believe in God the Creator" is not the result of observing the world, in the same sense as we might say: "I know the earth turns round on its axis", because that only accounts for day and night; even though it appears to contradict the appearance that it's the sun that goes up and down. When we say: "I believe in", we are making a claim that this or that is what we commit ourselves to: we will stand by it, and we will live by it until our experience bids us reject it. If a humanitarian reformer declares: "I believe in the brotherhood of man", he is not saying: "I observe that men behave as if they are truly brethren to one another", for that would be patently false. Men don't behave as brothers, except to a limited extent and much history is of strife between people. But our reformer is quite entitled to say: "I believe in the brotherhood of man", meaning, in spite of all human behaviour, which contradicts it, I am committing myself to the certainty that if I work for the brotherhood of man I can count on some truth about human life, which, though obscured and thwarted, is a hidden but practical fact, that men at the deepest level are brethren under the skin. One other example: when the old lady wanting to tell you some home truth says: "I believe in speaking my mind", she is not stating a bare fact, she is telling you that this is the kind of behaviour she is committing herself to, for she holds it to be the best kind of attitude, even though there may often be a good deal of make-believe in her actual judgment of what "speaking my mind" may reveal.

Well then, what is the Christian committing himself to when he recites, "I believe in God the Father Almighty, Maker of Heaven and Earth"? We could answer in a set of general statements, which protect but do not express a living faith. For instance: the world is God's creation means first that the world is not self-sufficient. It has its existence and its character from a divine will. So has human life—and the human mind, which asks the question. An answer can only be approached in terms of a relation between this world and its divine ground. Older theologies put it this way: The world has been given a creaturely nature, which can be attended to without referring to God. That is the nature of our secular and scientific knowledge. I, as a creature, have a human essence, I am not just a drop in the ocean of divinity. And the wood of this pulpit has a vegetable essence, a certain independence in its nature. But there has to be added, according to this older theology, that all these creaturely beings, while they have their own nature, owe their existence entirely to the creative act of God. This we cannot tell by looking at them: it is an act of faith, which we make because we have other sources of knowledge besides those that come from our attention to the world. Something has been said to us about it in God's own way; this we call revelation.

Two other things about creation can be mentioned. One is that because the world is God's creation, the world is of God, but the world is not God. The principle of unity—that which makes the world a universe, is in God, not in the world itself. Men have often tried to find the meaning of the world somewhere in the world itself. The older Greek thinkers looked for that one thing of which all other things were different forms. One said it was water; another air; another fire. Nowadays people are inclined to look for the key to the world's meaning in some kind of process with a promise that the meaning will be disclosed when the process is complete, what the French Jesuit, Teilhard de Chardin, calls the Omega point.

The second thing about the world as a creation of importance for our faith is that the created world is made up of myriads of creatures, living and impersonal; and if creation is true each particular thing in the world has a significance for itself derived from its relation to God, not only because it is a bit of the whole. That is the basis of the Christian emphasis on the meaning and value of particular things. "Even the hairs of your head are all numbered". Especially, no human creature should be treated as a convenience or a nuisance for some greater cause or social system. Christianity has laid great stress on this value of things in themselves, as ends not only means; and this too is connected with the idea of creation. But enough of this theoretical description, for the Church did not arrive at the doctrine of creation by first thinking out these things.

The teaching of God as creator came in a different kind of language, dramatic, poetical. The Bible as we have it begins with utterances like this: "God said let there be light and there was light" and so with the earth and its place in the larger world; then the seasons, the stars, the animals, and central to all, man, who does the thinking. "God said", using an image of speech for God's creative act. In the Bible "word" meant not only expression but creative power. And when the seers of the Bible tried to distinguish between the unknown beauty of God, out of which all things come, and His creative action, other terms became used. In what is called the wisdom literature—it is the divine wisdom, which is used to convey the creative power of God. "I was by him as a master workman", it is written in the Book of Proverbs, speaking of the creative power of God as distinct from His inexpressed being. "When He prepared the Heavens I was there rejoicing in the habitable part of the earth and my delights were with the sons of men". You see, the nature of creation is never divorced from the problems and destiny of men. It was this creative wisdom of the Old Testament, which became named the Word—or Logos in St. John's Gospel. "The word was with God, and the word was God: all things were made by him". And then, there is no more clear expression of the close link between God as creator and God as saviour of men than in St. Paul's letter to the Colossians: he speaks of the Father "who delivered us out of the power of darkness and translated us into the Kingdom of the Son of His love, in whom we have redemption, the forgiveness of sins". And this message of salvation and rebirth is immediately linked to the creation of the world by God: "For in Him were all things created... and He is before all things and in Him all things consist". So the original notion of the world as God's creation was, as it were, an outflow from the message that God who is revealed as Father in Jesus Christ is in fact the very God from whom the world has its origin. Thereafter Christians and others have often attended to the meaning of creation in separation from the saving work of Christ. And that is quite legitimate, but the original link should not be forgotten. In fact in our worship we are reminded of the link. Take the hymn *Praise my Soul, the King of Heaven*, an act of adoration. To whom? Yes, to the Lord of Creation. "Sun and moon, bow down before Him, dwellers all in time and space". But the Lord of Creation is also the holy one we address in words like "Praise Him for His grace and favour"; "father-like He tends and spares us... rescues us from all our foes". The Creator is one with the Saviour.

And we also sing another kind of hymn altogether, by Joseph Addison, the English man of letters who lived at the end of the seventeenth century and the beginning of the eighteenth. It illustrates how the idea of creation takes its form from the intellectual atmosphere of a particular life. Addison was a contemporary of Newton; and all thinkers of the time were so impressed with the newly found regularity of the natural world that it was in terms of the physical harmony of the spheres that they found evidence of the world's creation. "The unwearied sun from day to day does his creator's power display". For these men the regularity of physical nature declared the divine reason, which created it. "In reason's ear they all rejoice and utter forth a glorious voice, forever singing as they shine, the hand that made us is divine".

When people have looked at the created world, they have been struck by that aspect of the world they were interested in or got excited about. We are all rather like that. In the same way when men have enquired what the created world said to them, they saw aspects of it, in which they had a concern. Addison's eighteenth century had the concern for the orderly working of the physical universe. Others have been more impressed with the disharmonies like ruthless nature, red in tooth and claw, and worried over the facts of suffering. Only a few years after Addison's ecstasy over nature's harmonies, Sydney Smith, the wit and Canon of St. Paul's, was fond of teasing his friend, Francis Jeffrey, Lord Advocate of Edinburgh, because of Jeffrey's perpetual criticism of everything: "I know what you think of the solar system", said Smith, "bad lights, planets too distant, pestered with comets, feeble contrivance. Could make a better with great ease". And so it goes on, men see in the world what impresses them.

For the Christian believer it is of intense concern that the creative power in the universe is the same as the God who meets us in our daily lives. We know in many ways how God shows Himself to us in our situation, and how our life in Christ helps us to live with a lot of unanswered questions. And when we have accepted Him as Lord of our life, we are then committed to regarding the universe as His work. Do the heavens still declare His glory? Will the heavens declare His glory only to those who already believe in Him? We cannot find by looking at the world more of God than we already know from other sources. And the other sources are all summed up in this: "God has beset us behind and before, and laid His hand upon us". This is intimacy indeed. When we have as our background knowledge the certainty that in Him we live and move and have our being, we can now and then bring that knowledge into the foreground, as we do when we affirm that He who dwells in light inaccessible is the Creator who is also our Father.

5. Christianising Our Sacrifices
A Lenten Meditation

"Wherefore do ye spend money for that,
which is not bread and your labour for that,
which satisfieth not?"
(Isaiah lv.2)

SACRIFICE by itself is not a Christian virtue. Many people now talk as if it were, and this is only a further example of debasement of the Christian coinage. There is perhaps not much harm in a word of religious origin coming to be used in a very secular way. My dictionary tells me that sacrifice in its first meaning is the offering to a deity, sometimes at the cost of life, and then gives as an example of one of its derivative uses the phrase we see in shops "surplus stock for sale at large sacrifice". I say there is not much harm in secularising a religious term, but it has the danger of putting down all losses for some gains as having the force of sacrifice in the religious sense. This is more of a fault in the pulpit and the parliament than in the market place, the field or the workshop. It leads to such evasions as the formula that if men are baffled by great social problems, then we must make sacrifices. And when the formula is delivered in the name of religion, this is called the Christian solution; it assumes that if men are prepared to make sacrifices for an object it must be a good object. And the habit has spread from the moral to the political platform, where it is frequently taken for granted that if someone or one set of people can be induced to give up something, then a desirable result will follow—an elementary error the beginner in logic will point out. Certainly the Christian knows that to do the will of God demands many renunciations, but it does not follow that all surrender of satisfactions makes for perfection.

Of course, the Old Adam in us knows quite well that he has got to put himself out and give up a good many things for the things he wants more. Readiness to accept sacrifices is as much a quality of the sinful self as one of the sanctified soul. Men have cut themselves with knives, they have made their children go through the fire, they have given the fruit of their body for the sin of their soul. They have made sacrifices for their own ends or in the service of false gods. Tyrants have often renounced marriage, love, wine and good living. I met one magnate, amassing power over millions of people, who lived on hot water and charcoal biscuits. And we have all made others pay for the misery we inflict on ourselves in the cause of our own merits. "The egoist" as Berdyaev says "is not always one who loves himself", he often torments himself and then takes a kind of revenge upon his neighbour. The bare fact that a man makes sacrifices is of no religious value whatever. Sacrifice— in the current sense of giving up something or accepting the loss of certain satisfactions is inherent in human life itself. We have to do it anyway, and our resentment of this is as much the material of sin as the transfiguring of it in Christ is the meaning of holiness. Lent is the season, in which we learn to Christianize our sacrifices.

The preacher quoted in our text from second Isaiah reminds the Jewish exiles in Babylon, on the eve of their return to Zion, that the sacrifices they have made in a strange land have been profitless, the money spent and the labour endured. He makes them the Lord's offer that if they accept His covenant and make the same sacrifices in the meeting place of God and man—then they will find that what they spend earns the bread that perishes not, and the efforts they make bring abiding satisfactions. That parable from biblical history suggests one way, in which members of the church can use the forty days of Lent to learn what Christianizing our sacrifices means, so that these become fruitful of freedom, love and holiness instead of being, as they so often are, the meat of bitterness, self-righteousness, enmity and resentment.

We must begin by looking at Christ in His sufferings—His passion, which means "having something done to one". It is the opposite of action, imposing oneself upon the world. But this is the outside of the picture. Behind and informing the passion of Christ, there is hidden, and unknown except to faith, the action of the living God. This is disclosed only to those who discern the other side of Calvary—the life risen from the dead; who know the passion of Christ to be the divine action. It is the action of God who is wholly free, who is not constrained by the world He created. In the passion of Christ who is defeated and killed, the divine power and love has hidden itself. God there submits His actions to man, and it becomes Christ's passion. His freedom accepts a constraint, which is not imposed by any necessity. It is *agape*, gift love, not need love.

Men, on the other hand, are constrained by two necessities: by their finite existence—there is the arithmetic of nature, which exacts a cost for every gain: and also, men are constrained by their share in a sinful world and their own disordered nature. These constraints we have to endure just because we are men.

The christianising of our sacrifices means offering these things, which we would endure anyhow—offering them in union with Christ in His passion. It means joining our inevitable servitude to His assumed servitude, so that ours can become the offering of a free heart. The endurance of our constraints can be made into a living sacrifice only when it is mingled with the divine freedom in Christ who meets us in our constraints to the uttermost.

Let us list same of the constraints, first the things that involve us in sacrifices just because we are creatures in this world. They are the things we endure because of our common human lot. At any time men must curb some demands in order to fulfil others. The child soon learns that if he spends his pocket money on this book he cannot have that toy. The young man or woman is fortunate if he or she learns in time that if they want a satisfying job, they may have to put up with a smaller income. People of noble aspirations often have to renounce one generous impulse in order to follow another. Then they have to deal with the problem of perplexity. Sometimes to do an actual small good means curbing the vanity satisfied in contemplating a big one.

The seed for next year's sowing must not be eaten up this year. There are losses inherent in mortality, the drudgery, which precedes every attainment of excellence in the arts or the sciences. There are the pains of thwarted purposes; and in conditions of insecurity there is the fear, the anxiety, the worry about the future. Even the comfortable can be troubled by doubt whether existence has any meaning at all. All these endurances are there more or less all the time; they are often borne bravely by men's natural fortitude and cheerfulness. But we cannot escape them. These burdens are not a free offering.

And now, on top of such constraints and sacrifices, which belong to our common human lot, there are to be added the things that Christian men endure because they are Christian. These include, of course, the exacting standards required by the Christian moral law; the uncomfortableness of having certainties, which are not communicable by the kind of thing outsiders recognise as evidence; the self-questioning of the Christian teacher, which arouses concern lest, having preached to others, oneself should be a castaway. There is the sense of sharing the common guilt of a sinful race; the burden of knowing the harm we inflict by the rough justice our best systems have to pit against chaos or counteract egoism: and when there are wars or fightings about, there is the load, which seems heavier at accepting safety at the cost of other people's lives, than if we were throwing away our own. For the sensitive Christian conscience there is the terrible knowledge how dangerous it is to be on the right side; it conceals and excuses so much human self-satisfaction. There is the burden of choice: doubts whether a projected action is right or wrong; perplexity as to what is God's will when one is confronted with two possibilities, both of which seem morally excellent but are incompatible. Most of these burdens men could escape if they could stop being Christians and could stop seeing humanity in the light of Christian insight. They are the tribulations that arise "because of the word", as it says in our Lord's explanation of the parable of the sower: "he that receiveth the seed into stony ground is he that heareth the word and immediately with joy receiveth it; but when tribulation or persecution ariseth because of the word, immediately he is offended".

The religious writer in Denmark of a century ago, Søren Kierkegaard, meditating on this passage, says that he has heard many sermons upon it. "Those preachers", he writes, "preach quite Christianly about the necessity of passing through many tribulations to enter the kingdom of heaven. But listening more closely, one discovers with surprise that these many tribulations are nothing else but illness, financial difficulties, anxiety for the year to come, what one is to eat, or anxiety about what one ate last year and has not paid for, or the fact that one has not become what one desired to be in this world, or other such fatalities. About these things one preaches Christianly, one weeps humanly, and one crazily connects them with Gethsemane. In case it were through these many tribulations one enters into the kingdom of heaven, the heathen also must enter into the kingdom of heaven, for they also pass through the same". Precisely, this second kind of constraint or tribulation comprises those, which men could avoid by ceasing to be Christian. They are because of the Word. But, having set our hand to the plough we cannot turn back. So, in a way, we of the Christian faith cannot avoid even these constraints.

We have then two bundles of weight to carry: those we have to bear as men and those we bear as Christian men. And there is only one thing to do in order that this double burden—the burden of our common human lot and the added burden of our Christian commitment—may become in us one with Christ's burden, with which He redeems the world. That is to add a third constraint to our already heavy-laden souls. I mean we take on some task or renounce a pleasure or endure some privation, in no case because such an act is required by duty or need. It is not demanded by morals or the state of the economy; it does not help the national effort; it has nothing to do with a career. In the eyes of the world, it does no good to anybody. One of the old-fashioned exercises, in which we give up something in Lent, will do. It will be a simple act of our spiritual freedom, not compelled by any necessity. A small part of our life becomes a free offering and it can be made with a flourish, and not with misery. Then we shall find that the sacrifices we have to make as humans and the burdens we have to carry as Christians, they too in a mysteriously real way become transfigured into something freely offered for the love of God. The leaven of uncompelled charity leavens the lump of our necessities and constraints. If we do something we need not do, and if it be done in love and reparation, then what we have to do can become a willing and a Christian sacrifice. We find that Christ's yoke is indeed easy and His burden light.

6. The Representative Offering
Passion Sunday

"I delivered unto you first of all that which I also received,
how that Christ died for our sins
according to the scriptures".
(1 Corinthians xv.3)

THIS WEEK [The week beginning 15 March 1970] there is to be a grand service in Westminster Abbey to celebrate the completion of a new English translation of the Bible. Is it not remarkable that such a colossal enterprise of scholarship and publication can happen at a time when the Christian faith is declared to have lost its hold upon most English people? Is it not then a good moment to ask the question, What is this Bible, still probably the best seller of all the world's literature? The late Dr. Austin Farrer when he was asked fifteen years ago to make a selection from the Holy Scriptures, called A *Short Bible*, which appeared as a Fontana paperback, said that to write an introduction to the Bible would be like writing an introduction to English poetry from King Alfred to Queen Victoria. But there would be this difference, that the Bible is valued and read for the sake of a single theme. The scriptures of the Old and New Testament are included under a single name for no other reason than this, that through them the person and work of Jesus Christ are understood.

Today is Passion Sunday, calling to us for a renewed grasp of the sufferings and death of Christ as an act, by which men can be saved from the dominion of sin and evil, an act, which is guaranteed as a divine act by the Resurrection. That fulfilment however is known only to the disciples, whereas the crucifixion was public knowledge. Now, there are many strands in the cord, which gives a unity to the Bible narrative, and I wish to isolate only one this morning. It is the one, which interprets the Passion of Christ as a perfect offering.

The Old Testament is about a people who had an intense sense of their dependence upon God, not only for their religion but fundamentally for their physical and historical existence. In spite of repeated betrayals and backslidings on their part, they were never allowed by God to cut right away from the conviction that all they were and all they had was a gift from Him and must be used in His service. This consciousness of a debt owing to the Lord is the basis of the Hebrew sacrifices, crude and savage as those sacrifices seem to us, with the most awful one of all, Abraham's readiness to slay his son. This consciousness gives the Old Testament sacrifices a character quite different from the ritual offerings of other ancient peoples. For the people of the old covenant something had to be done for two reasons, one to acknowledge before God that for all their properties, life and powers they were beholden to God who gives it all, and secondly to remind themselves repeatedly that they were perpetual debtors to Him. How was this sense of indebtedness to be expressed? Not just by pious thoughts and words, but by certain acts. Those acts took the form of what may be called "representative offerings". Part of what man owned and used and valued was offered to the Lord, given a religious meaning, set apart from ordinary usage. The most obvious, and to us somewhat shocking, act of this kind was the slaying of animals, the creatures, sheep, cattle, goats, which were the material wealth of the Hebrew tribes. The first lamb born of the flock, but also the first sheaves of the corn harvest, the first loaf of bread baked, the first bundle of fruits from the trees; all these portions of what men lived by, were made the material of a religious offering, and were called "first fruits". Why? In order to acknowledge that the whole of people's natural existence and possessions are gifts, some portion becomes offered religiously. Otherwise men would forget that the whole is loaned from the Lord. St. Paul used this image of a representative offering when he said: "if the first fruit is holy, the lump also is holy". It is a refrain running through the Bible. In the book of Leviticus you find statements like this, "Ye shall eat neither bread, nor parched corn, nor green ears, until the selfsame day that ye have brought an offering unto your God", or in Proverbs, "Honour the Lord with thy substance, and with first fruits of all thy increase". Biblical religion has this kind of logic: if all men have and do was turned into ritual religion, then natural life would not go on as God intended; but if nothing were set apart as a special religious offering, men would treat their whole existence as their own and ignore that all their biological substance, their engineering and the powerful efforts of thought and science, can easily be turned to false and inhuman purposes. Today we are witnessing a world-wide alarm at the reckless misuse of the earth, on which we live.

The time came in Old Testament history when God through his prophets declared that the people's sacrificial offerings of their property were only acceptable as a token of their sense of dependence. But what He really requires is a life of complete obedience. Without that the former offerings were "vain oblations", empty performances. "What does the Lord require of thee but to do justly, love mercy and walk humbly with thy God". That is the second article in the logic of sacrifice. But what then, if the only acceptable offering is a life of perfect obedience to God's will, who can make it? "There is none righteous", cried Isaiah, "no, not one". There is no answer to that riddle in the Old Testament. The Passion of Christ is the answer, the act, by which the incarnate Lord, in the humanity He assumes, becomes the representative offering of the human race, which cannot make it on its own. It is as if the Lord said to mankind, you cannot make the only offering pleasing in my eyes, so here is the life of perfect obedience, given to you. It is God's own life carried through in the man Jesus Christ so completely that God the Son does the heavenly Father's will unto death. There is no swerving away from that holy obedience. But even if we grasp it at all, we are still left with a terrible plight. Is it not in a way wicked and immoral to rely on someone else's holiness, even though He, the Christ, be our representative? To stress this side of the Atonement is but half of the divine requirement, that half known in the scriptures as *Justification*, being accounted righteous by our faith in Christ's righteousness. What is this saving act of God's, of which all we can say is, "He died that we may be forgiven" for our unrighteousness we cannot overcome. How can I stand before God and say, there, He lived, unto death, in perfect obedience to the Father's will on my behalf, in my place, instead of me. If that were the whole truth, the truth of justification, then perhaps we could claim a grain of original righteousness in crying, I will not have salvation at the price of anyone else. But it is not the whole truth. Christ is not anyone else. We are one in Christ as we are one in Adam, as St. Paul was always saying. And the mystical union of the Christian and Christ is guaranteed by the further act, by which His perfect offering becomes something done not only *for* us, in our stead, but also something done in us and by us. That is the possibility of *sanctification* represented by the Last Supper, or the Holy Communion, when Christ shares His sacrificial offering with His people. His offering becomes their offering. The cross of Christ's Passion becomes our own, as our most moving Eucharistic hymns express it: we live it out as best we can. Bishop Rawlinson used to say the meaning of the Cross was not read into the Last Supper, it was read out of it. Christ assumes the role of the Passover lamb; He bore the sins of many outside the gate.

We know something in our regular act of worship of the idea of a representative offering. The whole of our time is God's time, for whom one day is as a thousand years and a thousand years as one day. But in order that we may live with that truth, even when we are occupied in work, recreation and thought, when our minds have to be on the job and not mooning about feeling devotional, in order that we may know in that hidden unconscious part of our life, that all time is God's, we set apart certain times, in which to be at attention before Him. The times of our prayers, in church and in private; and one day in seven is in a special sense the Lord's Day. That does not mean that the others are entirely our own time. "Seven whole days not one in seven" as an older hymn puts it, are indeed the Lord's time, but without the representative offering of those parts deliberately dedicated to Him, we lose the sense that the whole of our time is the Lord's time; and we get what we know as the secularisation of all life.

When we annually at this time salute the Cross of Christ as the material symbol of Christ's Passion, we can deepen our sense of its solemn meaning by recalling how Christian devotion has through the centuries celebrated it. While Passion means suffering and endurance, having something done to one, the passion hymns like *The Royal Banners Forward Go*, and *Sing My Tongue the Glorious Battle*, make sure we cannot miss the hidden victory wrought by Christ in His Passion. The note of triumph, of God's rulership, has been struck repeatedly in devotion to the actual wood of the cross, often called the Tree. "Oh Tree of Glory, tree of might". Nowhere has this victorious side of the Passion been more sublimely voiced than in an Anglo-Saxon poem of the eighth century called *The Dream of the Rood*, rood being the old word for the wooden Cross itself. [The poem has now received a new translation by Mr. Richard Hamer in a paperback edition called A *Choice of Anglo-Saxon Verse* (Faber and Faber)]. The central part of the poem is in words spoken by the actual Cross itself. They tell of the Saviour in His endurance, also deliberately conquering:

> "Then the young hero (who was God Almighty)
> Got ready, resolute and strong in heart,
> He climbed onto the lofty gallows tree,
> Bold in the sight of many watching men.
> When he intended to redeem mankind".

But before recording in his dream this utterance of the wooden cross the poet speaks of it in his own words:

> "The Ruler's tree was worthily adorned
> With gems (the nail heads); yet I could see beyond that gold
> The ancient strife of wretched men, when first
> Upon its right side it began to bleed... I saw that lively beacon

Changing its clothes and hues, sometimes it was
Bedewed with blood and drenched with flowing gore,
At other times it was bedecked with treasure.
So I lay watching there the Saviour's tree".

"Blood and gold"; Christ's saving work wrought for the misery and glory of man.

7. Not One World, but Two
Ascensiontide

"The Most High hath not made one world, but two".

THIS pronouncement from the apocryphal writing known as Second Esdras (vii.50) gives the biblical answer to one fundamental religious question. All religions can be identified by the way, in which they answer it. It is the question whether both the eternal world and the temporal world are real. And if both are real what is the relation between them?

The Christian Faith does not begin by putting the question in these terms. But it does imply an affirmation about such things when it proclaims the events set in motion by the coming and going of Jesus who is called the Christ, events, which have a central significance both cosmically and historically. When the New Testament speaks of His ascending into heaven and when the Church's creed adds that He sits at the right hand of the Father, they describe happenings that take place across the border-line between the temporal and eternal worlds, between this existence of ours, which involves us in time, in change, in history, in struggle, and a reality behind it, which is timeless but which gives a meaning to all temporal events, which is changeless but engenders change, itself unmoved but the burning source of creative and healing energy.

Two Worlds

We will now consider first why it is necessary to believe in the two worlds, second, how the Ascension of Christ declares their distinctness and connection, and third, what this means for a faith to live by. It is necessary to believe that both eternity and history are real. You may hold that the unchangeable origin and substratum of things is the only reality, that the world of events, of variety, of particulars and distinctness—that this is illusory or a bad joke or a misery or a lapse from true being. Creation and history then become a fallen condition and salvation consists in being free of it. This is the theme of some Greek philosophy, of much eastern religion and of a modern book like Aldous Huxley's *Perennial Philosophy*. To adopt this attitude is to disbelieve that the Eternal God created a real world of things, of movements and of critical turning points, an insistence, which the Bible makes by assuming that the created order is intended and is not in itself a distorting panorama of eternity. But you are probably not likely to be attracted by this denial of the reality of the temporal unless it be by a wistful rebound from the characteristic working dogma of the modern world, which is its precise opposite. This contends that only the temporal world is real; all is in flux, or becoming. Any notion of a reality transcending the world process, behind the scenes as it were, is regarded as a projection or ideology, or as a refuge from the rough and tumble of our temporal existence. On this view the world process has its meaning within itself, such as an undated millennium in the future, or some national or cultural way of life in the present or of a lamented past. If there is a God, He is entirely immanent, the dynamo driving the cosmic machine. This dogma has a spiritual dress in idealist thinkers like Hegel, a materialistic one in revolutionaries like Marx and a patchy cloak of spiritual ideas and materialist aims in the evolutionary moralism of the late liberal era.

What has God to do with the temporal world? ask the ancients and the Easterns and some Western idealists. If God is all in all, the high and lofty One that inhabiteth eternity, what has He to do with change and history, with this man end that insect, with this society, in which we toil and moil, where little systems have their day, and men try again and again to make a home for their souls and bodies after each breakdown of their constructions? Or conversely, when the fascination or the seriousness of life in the world shuts out all other perspectives then men ask how can this multifarious, untidy end cruelly baffling setting of our existence have its meaning in some living God "with Whom is no variableness or shadow of turning". Is not this notion of an eternal reality—non-moving at its centre—is this not an escape, an illusion of rigidity to save us from getting quite involved in the struggles of our time?

When the scriptures declare that the Most High has made not one world, but two, when the Church affirms in its creed that God is maker of Heaven *and* earth, something is said, which may not be mentally satisfying, but which safeguards a living faith and prevents men from mistaking what they can define and handle for the world, in which they are placed, for this has always dire results. One of these results is to seek the principle of unity in the world itself somewhere: in matter, in reason, in vitality, the libido, this culture or empire, that race or this messianic class. There must of course be a source of unity, or there would be no universe, no thought or science; but if the point of unity is sought in the world process itself, an idolatrous image of the eternal God is set up more seductive than Nebuchadnezzar's image because not so recognisable. There is today a widespread tenet that belief in an eternal world makes for servility, excuses injustice and deflects energy from worldly tasks. Lenin, for instance, wrote to Maxim Gorky: "The idea of God always benumbed and dulled the social sense by substituting the dead for the living, being an idea of servitude". It is true that much other-worldly religiosity has been a refuge from responsibility in this world; but on the other hand belief in men's link with eternity has often stimulated their efforts on earth by relieving them of the crushing despair that follows from desperate concern about results. And faith in a terrestrial fulfilment can be as much of an anodyne as a bad kind of flight to the skies. When dreamers of world peace despise lesser measures of international decency; or reformers resent smaller moves than their total programme towards a little more humanity and justice, then sublunar faiths are, as much as bad religion, what Charles Kingsley called opium for the people. Many disbelievers in the eternal world are deficient in concern for their fellows' welfare. In order to work for a better future in this world it is not enough to disbelieve in the other.

When men seek for meaning in a single track world they are asking for tyranny and often making for it, even with a goal of liberty in their hearts. George Santayana described such a one in his novel *The Last Puritan*:

"How Oliver hated picnics with the messy food and waste paper and empty bottles and loud merriment and tussling and amorous episodes improvised on the grass! Yet when necessary he put up with it all gallantly and silently... His imagination wasn't lordly and firm enough to set up a second world over against this one, and positively believe in it. He distrusted doubleness, but he couldn't admit chaos, and in order to escape chaos without imposing any fictions or any false hopes upon mankind, he would have been capable of imposing no matter what regimen on us by force... I think I know what Oliver's secret was, common enough if you like and even universal, since it was simply the tragedy of the spirit when it's not content to understand but wishes to govern".

A Fatal Mistake

Here is another dangerous consequence of refusing to submit to the reality of two worlds. You confuse them and make an absolute out of a slice of this relative shifting existence. The German philosopher Fichte in his *Reden an die deutsche Nation* said that man is made for an eternal end and is not inwardly content with a more limited one. But he used this truth to tell his compatriots that the individual person must therefore find his purpose and significance in the life of his *Volk*, for that, he averred, has an eternal life. You see what an easy but fatal mistake this can be. The race lasts much longer than the individual on earth, but the race still belongs to the temporal world; and if you give it the supreme value of the eternal you have to subordinate the person to the larger wave of temporal succession. All oppressions are of this nature. Man has an inalienable link with the eternal world of God and Heaven, but when he objectifies its pull upon him and makes absolute something in his temporal existence, in the end he loses his freedom. An alleged heaven on earth is easily another name for hell. And now, once more, the two worlds mean that things and events in history are under judgment by something outside history. That is really the concern of the writer of our text in Second Esdras. He is not concerned with a correct philosophic attitude; he has to proclaim an apocalypse, a secret about history revealed only to those who can live in it with the pivot of their lives in the eternal world now. For one thing, reality cannot be reduced to a harmonious whole for the convenience or pride of man, nor can mere success in time justify an act in history. Every thing and event has to be validated by its quality now, that is to say by the kind of mark it makes on the mirror of eternity and not only, or principally, by what it leads on to in the future.

All this, of course, is not the original language of Christianity. That language is about historic events, which disclose that they have an eternal reference, occurring as they do only once in time and space. The language is that of a cosmic drama. One of the main acts of that drama is the Ascension of Christ, though the records of it in the New Testament seem meagre, incidental and almost casual. "It came to pass while He blessed them, He parted from them, and was carried up into heaven", writes St. Luke, who adds, in the Acts of the Apostles, "a cloud received Him out of their sight".

The Ascension a Natural Ending

The Ascension of Christ into heaven comes into the drama incidentally, as it were, as a pledge that He who has entered the human arena belongs to the eternal world, not by reward or grace but by nature. He rises, not as Elijah in chariots of fire, but by the inward power of belonging to the Godhead. The bare fact is recorded without all the signs and prophecies and commotions that make up the Christmas story, or the gloom and terror and earthquakes that darken Calvary, or the trembling joy and nervousness of the disciples certifying that the Lord has risen. The Ascension is a natural ending. It ends that phase of what we may call, with proper reverence, the divine enterprise, in which the flesh of Christ stands for and subsumes our creaturely existence. It is not the end of God's restoring work, for after it comes the new history born of the Holy Spirit, the Church, within and alongside and cutting across the old history.

The glorious mystery of the Ascension, which confirms that He who had come belongs to the eternal realm, is described in figures of speech drawn from the temporal world. "He ascended", as if He went up in space. So our halting and jibbering language has to utter the fact that His involvement in the turmoil of world history is over and that He belongs elsewhere. "He sitteth at the right hand of the Father", as if in a position of space and in a bodily posture. But this is to mutter out of our tied tongues, that He who came as Saviour, who was rejected of men, enduring the contradiction of sinners in order that the unlovable may be loved, that it is He who wields the divine power of ruler and judge. A ruler sits in the seat of authority. Had He not said "All power is given unto Me in Heaven and earth"? It had to be said that the *agape*, the love given gratis without deserts, manifested in Him who became that one man and died, Jesus the Christ—it had to be said that that loves comes from Him who has sovereignty over all creation. This had to be said or else we should have to choose between a powerless but benevolent superior being who totters with this crumbling world, or an all-powerful lord of creation who only kept it straight by making it automatically register His will, like an infallible clockwork.

Therefore, the sovereignty of Christ has to be proclaimed as the sovereignty of Him who hid that sovereignty in the human Jesus of Galilee and Calvary. It is not that the primal source of all things whom we call God the Father—unknown as Father until so revealed in the Son—it is not that the lordship of the world passes from Him to the eternal Son. Rather, it is that this lordship, this sovereignty in sustaining and judging, is exercised in the Son. Nor is it that Jesus, whose flesh of this woman the eternal creative Word assumed as its vehicle, who lived at this period, who suffered under that regime, with a date and an address on earth, of the substance of our race, who carries our evil as if it were His own and transmutes it into a tool of grace—it is not that this One achieves a sovereignty at His Ascension not held before, or put aside for the time of His lowliness. No, the Ascension is neither an achievement of Christ's nor the happy ending of a sad story. It manifests—or draws the curtain open to show what has been hidden—that this is His place yesterday, today and for ever. He always sits on the right hand of the Father. He is now known as so doing. The cloud that received Him out of their sight was a veil that hid the other veil, the veil of His flesh, that, which had concealed His lordship in the love of the human Jesus and Him crucified. He who observed the sabbath and who was hanged on a tree for claiming to be Lord of the sabbath while looking as one who had to observe it, His lordship over it is now acknowledged.

Some of His own cryptic oracles now gain verisimilitude. "I came out from the Father, and am come into the world, again I leave the world and go unto the Father" (John xvi.28). It has been said by Karl Barth that the Ascension is the last of the appearances of the risen Christ and the first of the Church. So, while we are listening to the scriptures without straining to find in them the echoes of our own cogitations—really listening—let us see what the Ascension meant to the first men of the Church. St. Peter in his first Epistle attributes to the power of the Resurrection the believers' ability to please God in their temporal existence "with a good conscience", and without putting away the flesh. And the warrant for this is that He who rose from the dead is the same who "is on the right hand of God, having gone into heaven; angels and authorities and powers being made subject unto Him" (1 Peter iii.21–22). For St. Paul it is the same, but his emphasis in the Epistle to the Ephesians is that his readers may know the renewing power of Christ in themselves by enlightenment about Christ's calling, which is to sit far above all rule and authority and power and dominion, in things spiritual and worldly. When he wrote to the Church in Rome, it is the God who freely gives us all things, including our justification, whom Paul preaches. This grace is ministered to us through "Christ Jesus that died, yea rather that it was raised from the dead, who is at the right hand of God, who also maketh intercession for us" (Romans xiii.34).

At the Ascension Christ's historic career came full circle; but a new fact has been brought about. Not just the eternal Word, but that Word bodied in the manhood of the historic Jesus, this it is, which ascended into the heavenly place. This Christ, whose eternal patria and status are now declared, brings into them the integuments of historic existence, which He assumed. It is the manhood that rises, not a soul released from a cage. Christ crosses the line between the world of temporality and the timeless energy of eternity, with the marks of our temporality and the wounds made by our idolatry of it. The ascended Christ acts as the eternal priest by reigning in the humanity. It was this humanity of ours, which the Creator designed in His image in order to keep creation as a reflection of His Glory, and it is this same humanity of ours, which seeks to dominate instead of representing the creation. But in Christ manhood finds again the priesthood it has forfeited. Humanity is taken up, not spiritualised away.

Saving Insight into an Enigma

We have considered the Ascension of Christ as giving to the Christian a saving insight into the enigma of the two worlds. I would not have you think this is the only importance of the doctrine. But to view it in this light does serve to show Christian Faith to be an affirmation of the nature of existence and this is more potent in enhancing humanity's life than a religion that is primarily a moral fillip. I will conclude by telling of one or two consequences of living by the faith expressed in the Ascension of Christ.

Those whose religious observance is moulded by the cosmic drama of redemption and who follow the Church's seasons, are glad to have discovered this dimension of their existence—this regenerating movement that runs from heaven to earth and back again. They know thereby that they are not completely immersed in the two other movements of their earthly existence: the cyclical rhythm of nature and the irreversible determinisms of history. Humanity has sought *freedom* from the closed rhythm of nature by making history; it has then found itself shackled by the determinism of its historical creations—societies, states, economic and technical constructions and fled back to nature for breath. Living in these two constituents of the temporal world, nature and history, Christians need not either submerge themselves in them or seek to contract out of the challenges they represent. For they now see both nature and history—contradictory as they seem to one another—as pointing to a reality behind them both, for neither can be accounted for as a department of the other. Each cycle of nature is not merely repetitive and each span of history is not merely a link between past and future. Each has a vertical reference and can be found to have significance—nature by being sacramentally considered as the vestment of the eternal priesthood, and history apocalyptically as the sphere of momentous decision and judgment. The Lord of history is also the Creator of nature. Who would have known that, but for the biblical emphasis upon God as the Lord of this tiresome people, as one and the same with Him who made all things by His naming Word? Moreover, all times are significant times because they are related not only to what precedes and follows but to the crucial historic times of Jesus the Christ, which times, as we are reminded by the New Testament, in some real way anticipate the last day, when the temporal order is judged and eternity enfolds time. So this moment of ours and every other moment is a moment of eternity as well as of time. We live under the sign of the fullness of time, which is its termination. In the words of G.K. Chesterton's *Ballad of the White Horse*:

> "The end of the world was long ago,
>   And all we dwell today
> As children of some second birth
> Like a strange people left on earth
>   After a judgment day".

Precisely because there is an eternal world alongside of and penetrating this world of time and succession, Christians know and live by the faith that this time, which is the manner of our existence, is no mere string of happenings, but a drama of significant acts.

I need not therefore be too heavily concerned that I cannot see nor control the results in nature and history of my present doings. With Newman, I need not ask to see the distant scene, for this one step is taken, not that I know for sure where it may lead me or any successors, but having learned to recognise the echo it must make in the courts of heaven where Christ hears and assesses. The Ascension tells me I can find the right way of living in the present moment.

Ascension Day is, so to speak, the festival observed for the Lord's own sake: we rejoice for what He is and for Himself for once in a year, a year marked mostly by our commemoration of what He does. To know the Lord for Himself, not only for what He means to us, is the achievement of real conversion. In prayer it means contemplation of God's being, as the foundation of our recognising His acts for us and in us and of our conforming to them.

Therefore a revival of contemplative prayer and a restored public observance of Ascension Day would serve to keep open the possibility of men today recovering the Christian setting of their existence as the interaction of the eternal and temporal worlds.

8. The Spirit, Divine and Human
Whitsunday

"Who among men knoweth the things of a man
save the spirit of the man, which is in him?
Even so the things of God, none knoweth,
save the spirit of God". (1 Corinthians ii.11)

EVERY now and then a religious writer says that what we badly need is a good book about the Holy Spirit. Yes, writings about the Holy Ghost are apt to be curiously difficult and unsatisfactory. This sermon is no exception. But I wish to say why it will always be so. There will never be a convincing account of the Holy Spirit, not only because like the Father and the Son, the Holy Ghost is "incomprehensible". We cannot get our minds round it in order to give it a definition. That does not mean that they cannot in some way be known. "We speak God's wisdom in a mystery, that which has been hidden", writes St. Paul—but God revealed them through the Spirit, "for the Spirit revealeth all things; yea, the deep things of God". When the poet Gerard Manley Hopkins was asked by a friend what be meant by a mystery, he wrote in a letter, "By a mystery, I mean not a definite uncertainty, but an indefinite certainty". A conviction that cannot be put in a formula or proposition. But now, with the Holy Spirit we have an added puzzle. The early Church theologians, in order to do justice to all the facts implied by the new life of the Christian body, had to find some way of speaking of God acting in three modes; they spoke of God the Father as the hidden source of all things, unknown, except when revealed as creator and saviour by God the Son, and there revealed as Fatherly. The seers and thinkers of the Church have therefore sought to fathom the mystery of the Godhead in two ways. They have tried to infer something of God from His creation, the world; this effort is called "Natural Theology"; and then also they have listened to what He has disclosed of His nature in the scriptures, its prophets and lawgivers and supremely in the disclosure of His inner being by God the Son, the Christ, who took flesh in the historic Jesus. This is called revealed theology. In both cases something is offered to the Christian mind from outside it. Something of the nature and action of God can be appropriated and regarded as objects of men's search. You will notice that this search is described in various metaphors taken from our human faculties, seeing (the vision of God) or hearing His word, or thinking appropriately in adoration and reverence. It's a kind of moving out to grasp something that is there to be grasped as an object of awareness, even though the grasp is so very unsteady.

But the puzzle about the Holy Spirit is that here is God acting not as an object of our search, but in the search itself, starting it and carrying it out. That is why there is such a bewildering variety of descriptions of the word of God the Holy Spirit in the scriptures and the literature of Christendom. No description is possible, no perception can help, because the perception is what we are trying to perceive. Most of the language about the Holy Spirit is not a revelation of Himself; He is a power to perceive and appropriate other aspects of the Godhead. Listen to the phrases: "He, the Holy Spirit shall glorify me. He shall testify of me. He will bring to your remembrance all that I have said unto you". These are the words of Jesus. For St. Paul the test of the Holy Ghost is that man is brought by Him to the feet of Christ. "If any man have not the Spirit of Christ, he is none of His". It is by the Holy Spirit that men acknowledged Jesus as Lord, as having an absolute claim on them through and through. We may note that the New Testament less frequently speaks of the Spirit being in a man, but more strongly of the Christian man being "in the Spirit" or "living after the Spirit".

Let us try some similar puzzles from ordinary life, in order to see why the Holy Spirit is such an enigma. We look at a tree and we see it; what we do not see is the act of seeing, and the light, by which we see is not itself seen. We listen to music or speech, in appreciation or disapproval, and we attend to the player or a speaker and to the mind of the performer. But if we attend to our own activity of listening or looking we lose what is conveyed to us. Similarly, we cannot really look at the movement of the Spirit, just because it is the power, by which we do the looking. Once more, words can be said to you, to which you do not really listen. Some talk is like that: it never becomes a conversation. Others look as if they are listening, but they are thinking of what they want to say next, the moment you draw a breath. They receive sounds, but there is no real hearing. Further, if I take up a book on military strategy or gaze at a score of orchestral music they say nothing to me, for I am not initiated into the subject; I am not educated in these spheres. I am not, as people say today, on the same wave-length as the military expert or the composer. I am not open to what they express.

The language of the divine action is not natural to us like our mother tongue; we have to learn to listen to a language about a layer of reality, from which we are estranged. So to the man of Christian faith, God not only discloses something of Himself in His creation and salvation through God the Son. He also gives the Church the gift of hearing what is there said, to continue, I'm afraid, these inadequate metaphors drawn from the experience of sight and hearing. That gift of receiving is the work of the Holy Ghost, as it is described in the New Testament. He makes the man who believes open, receptive to the word. "Now we have received", writes St. Paul, "not the spirit of the world, but the spirit, which is of God, that we might know the things freely given of God".

Now we may turn to one of the most telling utterances about the Spirit, namely the passage I have chosen as the text where St. Paul refers by the same name "spirit" to two different things, the spirit of God and the spirit of Man. "Who knows the things of a man except the spirit of man, which is in him. Likewise, the things of God no one knows except the Spirit of God". The distinction is important, because the most common and dangerous modern religious error is to confuse the spirit of God with the spirit of man, or it may be added (which makes things worse) the spirit of man at its highest. What is the force in this expression "the spirit of man", which knows the things of man? I can only take it as naming the knowing self, the central reality, to which all one's activities or experiences belong. We call it by the same name "I" with regard to ourselves. This self, this ego, this I, is itself a mystery; it can never be an object of consciousness, because it is the ultimate subject. It looks outwards and cannot squint round to see itself. To use philosophical language, it is always a noumenon, never a phenomenon. It is therefore called the spirit. I said it looks outward never at itself: but outward means not only on the external activities of the human soul. Men can pay attention to thought (and, following Descartes, mistake thought for the self); they can become aware of feelings, hopes and fears in themselves and others and become practical psychologists. They can observe themselves making decisions or failing to make them. These are all parts of the inner life, which we can call the Soul, touching the experience of our bodily life and our contact with things outside. But the self, which has these experiences, is that mysterious reality we can best call the human spirit. The human being is a self-centred creature. It is a part of his being as created, it is the image of God in man, not a moral but a metaphysical image. Therefore he has will, and intelligence, ideals, causes, ventures, emotional surges and religious experiences. By this spirit-centred structure man stands over his place in Nature, confronts it and makes science, he stands over the process of history and makes laws and political systems. These are real expressions of the spirit of man reaching out and beyond himself. But they do not make him good or holy, or righteous, or religious; they make him human. The human spirit is very powerful, but it is not thereby the divine spirit. And the human spirit can lead amazingly into the arms of Satan if its works are not brought into subjection by the Holy Spirit. The spiritual urges of man are the source of the best and the worst in human life. The greatest villains in history have been idealists from Herod the Great to Hitler. Therefore the human spirit must never be confused with the Divine spirit. It must be submitted to Him.

Because of the possible confusion of human and divine spirit there is something ta be said for occasionally using the old English term "Holy Ghost" for spirit of God, at the risk of suggesting a spook or a wraith. Our English translations of the New Testament make the difference by spelling Holy Spirit with a capital S and the human spirit with a small one. However it is expressed, the difference is colossally important for two reasons. First, because the human spirit can make achievements and disasters; this does not by itself make the works godly. Secondly, because religious experience does not always bring men to union with God, it can often remain man-centred. Then people mistake their own spiritual vibrations for the action of the Holy Ghost and chatter about spiritual values.

Having stressed the distinction between the human and Holy Spirit, I must add that in Christian thought there is an analogy between them. The writer of Proverbs calls the spirit of man "the candle of the Lord searching all the inward parts", as if it were a little light lit by a big light. An image anticipating St. Paul, the spirit of man knows the things of a man. And in the second century the fathers of the Church were particularly concerned with the relation of human and divine spirit. One of them, Tatian, wrote to the Greeks: "We are acquainted with two kinds of Spirit, of which one is called soul and the other is greater than soul—yet the soul is not without resource, because it possesses an affinity with the divine Spirit and ascends to such regions as the Spirit leads us". And Irenaeus, who did not altogether agree with Tatian on other matters, makes the same point: "That which makes a man alive and soulish (ψυχικός) is quite different from the life-giving Spirit that makes him spiritual (πνευματικός) meaning informed by the Holy Spirit".

Well now, the distinction I am wearying you with is not only a matter of understanding what earlier Christian thinkers have made of it. It concerns very much the situation of mankind today. Because the human being is a spirit-centred creature, all his activities, beyond satisfying his bodily needs, proceed from that inner power of spirit in him. Man does not eat or make love or design computers as an instinctive biological creature. So when Christian believers get worried at the growing secularisation of life where more and more sections of existence are attended to without any reference to God or religion, or when they get alarmed about possible catastrophe of a misguided world, they are quite wrong to say it is all because we are too materialistic. It is rather that the spirit of man, because of his enormous powers to make a world, tends to disregard the laws and limits of his own being. It is the human spirituality in a spacious independence of the Holy Spirit. It is idolatry, not materialism.

What about Pentecost in all this? The strange happenings described in the second chapter of Acts, are called the Descent of the Holy Spirit. They are clothed in Old Testament imagery: the tongues as of fire, and the noise of wind. The devout Jews from all parts of the ancient world gathered in Jerusalem heard the Apostles speak in dialects strange to themselves, in languages of those of far-flung colonies, from which the pilgrims came. Whatever we may make of this ecstatic occurrence, something took place, which produced a new kind of unity—not rooted in a common territory, or civil society, or language, or custom—a living bond, which spread over their differences and separatedness. St. Peter spoke however in his own tongue when he explained that the foreign tongues, which the disciples uttered, were not due to drunkenness, but were uttered in some way as a fulfilment of what the old prophets foretold, and that the fulfilment was a renewed presence of the ascended Christ. This gathering into one body of diverse human material has been regarded by the Christian Church as its own birthday. The Holy Spirit makes the Church. He is the divine action uniting believers, and not the divine action, which informs all men. The principle, which informs all men, is God the Son, the Logos, the Word: the one who lighteth every man. The human race is in a sense one. God made of one all the nations of the earth. Theologically speaking all men are made in the configuration of the Christ, but that does not make them Christians; to become Christian they must be shown what they are and that is the work of Holy Spirit. The works of the Holy Spirit are legion, and cannot be listed completely. He has been known to believers as the power of truth and integrity. They that worship must worship in Spirit and in Truth. What do you make of "the sin against the Holy Ghost", of which Christ said it has no forgiveness? It is not the sin of misbehaviour, of making wrong moral choices, but the falsifying of language, of words, the breaking of the common bond of human communication. Dante places the falsifiers' words in one of the deepest circles of Hell.

The fruits of the Spirit are also an inner strength giving freedom from being crushed by the turmoil of our outer and private worlds—love, joy, peace, long suffering and so [on] as in St. Paul's catalogue of the gifts. He is the Comforter. Pre-eminently, the Holy Spirit is the principle of freedom. "If you are led by the Spirit you are not under the law", says St. Paul. "The spirit bloweth where it listeth", says the Lord himself. Here then is a strange thing. The Church is the creation of the Holy Spirit, yet time and again Christians have revolted against the Church in the name of liberty, they have sighed for a third epoch, the age of the Spirit, to escape from the constricting weight of Church power and organisation. And ages of the Spirit easily come to be equated with the spirit of the Age. Therefore the spirit of any age must be tested by the deliverance of God the Holy Spirit.

9. The Holy Trinity

"We speak God's wisdom in a mystery,
even the mystery, which hath been hidden".
(1 Corinthians ii.7)

THE COMPANY of academic heroes, who attend University Sermons with any frequency over a long period, must wonder at the occurrences every few years of discourses on the doctrinal formularies of the Church and on the heresies, which those formularies set out to withstand. I hope that what I have to say may serve to show that concern for doctrinal correctness—for orthodoxy in Christian thought, that is—and attention to these aberrations from it, which we call heresies—that these are not indeed the living substance of Christian Faith and Life, but are necessary protections of that substance from evisceration by attempts to explain the saving facts of Christianity by alien systems of thought. My thesis is in fact a direct contradiction of the widespread notion that to formulate doctrine and to arrest heresy is an attempt to rationalise the divine mystery. No, it is the other way round. When the human intellect has tried to translate the ineffable impact of the Divine action into language learnt in other spheres or in particular and local philosophies, the experience of the Church as the worshipping body of the redeemed has sensed that such attempts explain away the mysterious facts, on which it lives. And when the Church then counters those attempts, also by means of intellectual formulations, it is easy to see how people think that the Church regards these corrections as the substance of Christian Faith and Life.

If you look, for instance, at a document like the Athanasian Creed, so forbidding to many modern Christians, you will see in it a set of statements, which look rather like a legal document with clauses apparently contradicting one another and condemning views, which no one in his senses could possibly hold—like three Holy Ghosts. But it is also not unlike descriptions of the physical universe in modern scientific theory, where for example you have to assume a particle theory of light on Mondays, Wednesdays and Fridays and a wave theory on Tuesdays, Thursdays and Saturdays, and spend Sundays reflecting on some form of light behaviour that may require a third working hypothesis.

In theology, however, doctrinal statements are intended to protect from error, rather than to convey a living reality. They were never meant to express God's revelation of His own Nature and Activity; they came to be formulated because men so easily try to squeeze the truth of the divine mystery into some theory of their own. So St. Augustine called the creeds "fences round a mystery"—they are to stop people, especially those who have learnt a little Christianity and a lot of some system of thought, from explaining away the central facts, upon which Christian faith stands. The faith came first; then when sophisticated Christians tried to account for it in terms of some non-Christian philosophy, the doctors of the Church had to say at each aberration—not that way—or, it's not like that, it's like this.

When therefore critics of theology complain that in the creeds and formularies they are offered arid logic-chopping propositions instead of a living faith, when they tell us to abandon the formal language of theological definition and rely upon religious experience alone, they misconceive the relation between the formularies and the life of faith. They have just cause for complaint when Christian teachers speak and argue as if assent to credal correctness were the life of religion; but they then often draw the mistaken conclusions that the Church is hampered by such formulations and had better shed the load, or that creeds and doctrinal documents have no relation to experience of the saving acts of God.

Let us consider this relation. It is probable that Christian theology began when the early Christians had to come to terms in their minds with the facts of their new life in Christ. That was the one thing they knew—that somehow through the happenings concerning Jesus of Nazareth who is called the Christ, they had found a new life, experienced a second birth. This was a fact—a piece of religious experience if you like these terms—it was an event in themselves, which they could no more deny than they could deny their existence.

Speculation about this event probably did not begin until theorists gave an account of it, which would in some way deprive it of its living force. And so, it seems, there came about formulated propositions to safeguard the reality of the vital facts. One such assertion would be that He who had re-made them must in some way be the same He who had made them, the source and origin and the Lord of life and of the world's history. And again, He who had taken possession of them and bound them together in a new society, inside and running across the natural societies, to which they belonged, the Spirit, which made the Church, must be the same God who created and saved. Jewish Christians who had been taught that God's name was "I am"—needing no other, "sitting about the water flood that inhabiteth eternity"—Pagan Christians who had learnt from Greek thought that God was beyond the vicissitudes of history and nature—all were compelled by the threat of intellectual eclecticism, to come to some statement that did justice to the facts they knew—that the divine Source of all was He who was revealed in Christ the Saviour, and who had become the power of their own renewed nature. In such ways Trinitarian formulations were the *post hoc* protective affirmations of the facts. As early as St. Paul himself we find his still unsystematic doctrinal statements following on and not preceding, his basic certainty that in the law of the Spirit of life in Jesus Christ, he had found resolved that inner conflict of the two powers in him so piercingly described in the seventh chapter of Romans—that divided will so frustrating that it could be called "the body of this death".

But, you may feel, this is all very true and commonplace in connection with doctrine in its early stages. What about the controversies of later Councils and Church confessions? They surely are sheer obfuscations of real saving religion. Well, no; in them too the Church found it had to safeguard something vital. For instance, we are so used to the opening words of our Creed "Father Almighty; maker of heaven and earth"—they roll off the tongue as if we were uttering a commonplace—that we do not realise their tremendous import. At a time when the Church was in danger of invasion by a Hellenic idea that creation was a calamity—a view represented in our own day by neo-gnostics like Aldous Huxley—it had to be said that the created world is God's work—and not a lapse, or an illusion, or a bad joke. Therefore He is maker of Earth as well as Heaven. That error is not a prevalent one in the West today. We are rather inclined to think that the world process is the only reality, and the counter weight to this is the statement that God is also maker of Heaven, the eternal world behind and above the temporal one

Consider too the lapidary phrases of the Athanasian Creed, the Father is God, the Son is God and the Holy Ghost God. Are such statements really necessary? Well, yes. That the origin of all things is fatherly is not a piece of natural knowledge—it tells us that the impersonal forces in existence, so often cruel and indifferent to personal souls, are not original but derivative and fallen. As a powerful Jewish thinker, Erich Gutkind, has put it: "Nature is a grimace on the face of paradise, beneath which we can see the original features. We live among the ruins of the original world". Honest men may reject that picture of things, but if they do they are directly challenged by the statement "The Father is God".

That the revealer and saviour is God tells us that we must accept His own disclosure of the secret of His being and action from Jesus the Christ, and have our life broken and remade by His grace. It is vitally important for true religion that the saviour of mankind be known as of one substance with the Creator and not as another creature. For if one creature could save so could another, and men could make God fit some theory of their own, as they repeatedly try to do, and read in to the Christian revelation some scheme of their own for saving the world. Many are the tragedies of our fallen history, due to the idea that man can save man and that he is justified, often in the name of God, in subjecting his fellows to benevolent or oppressive tyrannies.

Once more, that the Holy Spirit is God tells us that the human spirit is in need of possession by the Spirit of God. To ignore this is perhaps the most widespread error of modern attenuated Christianity. To mistake the human, finite and sinful spirit for the Holy Ghost—and call it the divine spark or something like that—is the essence of man-centred religion. It leads to the characteristic and dangerous belief of our time that as the human spirit grows in knowledge and power over nature it gains in virtue, wisdom and love. Or it leads to mistaking our own spiritual vibrations for the divine action.

There was then something essential for lively Christian faith at stake in the formulations about the relations of the Son to the Father, and the Holy Spirit— formulations represented in particular in the Nicene period. But, is it so clear in connection with the later question of the relation of the two natures in the one person of Christ—the question, which received a provisional settlement at Chalcedon in 451. The issues there were much more internal to the thought of the Church than in the earlier controversies where the Christian revelation had to be safeguarded from deflections due to the effect of a heathen idiom being used—Greek thought language—to express, as Gilson says, an idea, which had never entered the head of a Greek philosopher.

At any rate the contestants in the fifth century disputes quite clearly held that this was no academic question for theological schools only, and this with such violence that each side was convinced that the other was not merely in error but must be quite perverse, in a way we do not understand. Yet, this kind of thing was said of Cyril of Alexandria by Theodoret, on the other side of the controversy. And it was not only a one-way traffic of invective. Read Cyril's letters to Nestorius, his chief opponent. You will see how it is assumed that theological errors were due to bad company; he must have consorted with horse-thieves and petty pilferers. It is appalling and strange to us to find great figures in an august controversy on deep religious questions, believing that different views must have something morally disgraceful about them. We may think poorly of them for it. But perhaps we had better note how seriously they took theology, moved not by pedantic concern for correct mental formulations, but by awareness that a whole attitude to life was at stake. They would not camouflage oppositions and make a pretence of unity lest the heathen be put off. They would not engineer a spurious agreement by some hedging document, like those dear to many religious leaders today, lest some be excluded. The things controverted mattered intensely. And what were they about? On paper, as it were, they were about the divine and human realities in God the Son; the two natures in one person; the perfect God and perfect man. But at bottom they were about the meaning of salvation. Of course, there were difficulties— due to the inadequacy of terms, and to the different meanings, which words convey to men of varying cultural and intellectual climates. Such difficulties are always present—that is why a religious superior told a subordinate the only document which avoids heretical interpretation is the Athanasian Creed, and it does so by contradicting everything it says as fast as it says it. But the difficulties are made unnecessarily acute when modern critics find fault with the metaphysical language because they want to interpret it psychologically, as you find it in Dr. Raven's strictures in his Gifford Lectures.

The problem dealt with at Chalcedon had been this: the Church at Alexandria, with Cyril at its head, stressed the unity of Christ, and would have nothing to do with words, which suggested two separate beings in one place—a divine and a human—which like the iron and clay in the toes of Nebuchadnezzar's image could, in Bacon's words, cleave but would not incorporate. And they thought that was what Nestorius was teaching. Nestorius was jealous for the real humanity of the Incarnate Christ, and seemed to say there were two separate sons of God—one natural, the Logos, the Word—the other adopted, Jesus the man. Nestorius shrank from the idea that He was *not* in all respects one with us men.

In this doctrinal battle one side was fearful that the other was endangering the unity of the person, the other side was fearful that the first was jeopardising the real incarnation by explaining away the conditioned limited being of Jesus of Nazareth. They were in many respects at cross-purposes, as Dr. Prestige and Duchesne have carefully shown—and the mixing of ecclesiastical and civil politics with doctrinal issues increased the bitterness generated. The Council of Chalcedon partly settled it—but as so often happens in these matters, each party thought the settlement favoured the other.

Now it is interesting to observe that the formula of Chalcedon—"two natures in one person" and the rest—has been severely handled by two modern scholar theologians, and that their rebukes contradict one another. Harnack in his *History of Dogma* says Chalcedon erred by explaining too much. "The true mystery", he wrote, "was contained in the substantial union of the two natures themselves. It was seriously damaged by being banished from its place here and when in place of it the conception of the union—a conception, which was supposed at the same time to involve a separation—was raised to the position of the secret of faith". Harnack had a prejudice against the West; he attacked Chalcedon and Rome for appearing to side with Antioch against the Greek Church, for, he maintained, the Monophysites were the true heirs of the theology of Athanasius.

But now, on the other side, we have Dr. Prestige declaring in his Bampton Lectures that Chalcedon failed through explaining too little. He writes:

> "Its definition of the Faith, served admirably as a warning against theological perversion, as a negative safeguard against heresy. But... the real intellectual problem, namely, how two distinct and complete natures are combined in one Christ, remained unsolved. In defining the two natures it speaks positively. But in defining their relations it speaks negatively.
>
> Christ is confessed in two natures, without fusing the natures together, without transmuting either in the other, without dividing Christ into two and without dissociating the natures from one another... It states admirably what Christ is not. On the constructive side it merely says He is one *prosopon*... one perceptible figure—one person—one objective reality or *hypostasis*".

It is, Dr. Prestige implies, negative, abstract, arid. But we may ask what else is human language to do—when the Church is threatened by intellectual robbery, which would snatch away the living substance of saving faith by false affirmations, what else is it to do but put up conceptual fences round the central mystery. We should agree with Harnack that the divine mystery must not be explained away—for then Christianity would lose its saving power. But we may then affirm that a formula like that of Chalcedon, by use of its many negatives, precisely does not explain it away—nor even explain it—it does preserve the hidden mystery.

The errors, which doctrinal formulations forbid, are the kinds of error, to which the human mind is always liable—man being what he is, a creature of two worlds—at the intersection of time and eternity, and also a subject as well as part of the objective world. Therefore any mental picture of his existence, whereby the mind seeks to overcome mystery (as it should, for that is its job) is always liable to do it by just the kind of aberration the heresies represent in theology. The human intellect, hating the loose ends of mysterious being, wants either to separate or identify, what reality in the rough has connected but not fused. The kind of formal mind, which in theology will confuse the persons or divide the substance of the Godhead, or confuse the nature or divide the person of Christ, will tend to make the same kind of mistake in other matters, cutting completely apart or merging into one, such things as religion and ordinary life, Church and society, sacred and secular, love and justice, faith and reason, action and contemplation, individual and community.

These pairs of real existences are given to us by the very nature of the created world; to accept them is to accept the mystery of existence. Christians relate them to the mystery of God's being, which, in the words of St. Paul, "none of the rulers of this world knoweth, for had they known it, they would not have crucified the Lord of glory. But unto us God revealed it through the Spirit, for the Spirit searcheth all things, yea, the deep things of God, unto whose ineffable majesty be ascribed all honour and glory, dominion and power, world without end".

III. GENERAL

10. The Soil of Virtue

"The righteous man shall be like a tree
planted by the rivers of water,
that bringeth forth his fruit in his season".
(Psalm i.3)

IN 1788 Richard Johnson sailed to Australia with the human contents of three English prisons; they included murderers, burglars, and forgers. On arrival he sent back to the Society for Promoting Christian Knowledge, asking for some literature on the art of being good. Why do we smile at this pathetic incident? Because the art of being good needs a much more prolonged growth than the purveying of moral advice can induce.

There is a frequent analogy made in the scriptures between religious and moral achievement and the processes of growth and vegetation. A deeper understanding of what is implied in likening development of virtue to the growth of a plant, might have put the modern Christian moralist more in the position of an attractive guide, and less in that of an interfering busybody, than has been the case. We are familiar with the torrent of moral exhortation poured out from platform, pulpit and press by those who have a remedy to offer for the plight of mankind. And in the area of the world, which is still in some way under the aegis of Christendom, these appeals for remedial behaviour have to be given a certain solemnity by being described as "Christian". Such appeals run from pleas for personal sacrifice to warnings like "society be good or the bombs will get you"—a form of secular terrorism, with which speakers seem now to be more at home than with the older threats of hell fire. But at the same time there is a growing doubt of the effectiveness of all this advice that men should pull up their moral socks in order to save humanity from the results of a society where the drift of things is not backing up the moral aims advocated. And this, quite apart from the fact that reliance upon moral exhortation as the main or the first word of Christianity, is a sure sign of decline in religious vitality.

The imagery used to illustrate the formation of character in the scriptures and in the Church, suggests that virtue does not come into being by bare acts of decision; it is rather the natural result of a process of growth, which brings forth its fruit spontaneously. The character is the product of a number of forces represented, in the imagery, by the soil, the sun, the climate and the tending, forces, which are at work behind the final result. When the Psalmist declares that the righteous man is like a tree planted by the rivers of water, bringing forth his fruit in due season, he is bidding us to consider righteousness as the fruit of an inner growth, nurtured by a culture not immediately moral. The virtues are the crops of plants, which grow in a certain soil and have their own proper setting. The Old Testament poets use this vegetation imagery, as we find it in the Book of Canticles, or in the song of Isaiah, which begins "My well-beloved hath a vineyard in a very fruitful hill". The New Testament employs similar nature symbolism. Christ asks: "Do men gather grapes of thorns or figs of thistles?"; He announces: "I am the vine, ye are the branches". St. Paul describes the Christian life as one springing from a new source. "If the root is holy so are the branches"; "it is not thou that bearest the root, but the root thee". More specifically, conversion to faith in Christ is likened to being grafted on to a new stem: "thou wast cut out of that, which was by nature a wild olive tree, and was grafted contrary to nature into a good olive tree".

All this should impress upon us that to exhibit the Christian virtues it is not enough to dwell upon their desirability. There has to be a tending of forces, which form the soul below the level of deliberate intention; if there is not, then any pumping up of moral energy will lead to despair and wretchedness. Whenever men have tried to inculcate the life of righteousness without the inner growth, of which it is the natural fruit, then morals have poked out aridly as mere command. When this happens morality has all the marks of an unlovely legalism; the devil will appear to have all the best tunes; moral leadership will look harsh and interfering; the Church will seem to be merely looking round to see what people are doing and trying to stop it, like the woman saying to her daughter: "Go and see what Johnnie is doing and tell him he mustn't". It would be unjust to attribute this bare prohibitive attitude to the Church at large, but it has appeared too much in such a light in recent centuries, especially in lands where the august virtues of puritanism, which for a short span were the fruits of a genuine religious culture, have degenerated into a set of moral inhibitions, with which to harass the worldly. On the other hand, the need for an inner growth from a soil and climate, which rear the moral virtues so that these operate without too much creaking effort, has been implied by the Church in its discipline of the spiritual life and in the dramatic and liturgical form of its worship, with the regular recital of Bible reading and with the enactment of the mystery of Christ's passion and resurrection, and with the ways of interior prayer. In pre-Christian Greek thought, as in Aristotle, ethics are not confined to the qualities of bare acts; they are also concerned with the fostering of a character, a nature, a disposition, making for a tendency, which builds up the good will. So we have the word "ethos" to describe the characteristic spirit of a community, whether civil or religious, which predisposes members to certain forms of habitual behaviour. Where ethics are restricted, in school or sect, to the moral quality of acts themselves, too often moral excellence is supposed to depend upon the difficulty in attaining it, as if life were primarily a moral obstacle race, prizes going to those who surmount the highest hurdles. "When we see a soul", wrote Ralph Waldo Emerson in his essay on Spiritual Laws, "whose acts are regal, graceful and pleasant as roses, we must thank God that such things can be and are, and not turn sourly on the angel and say 'Crump is a better man with his grunting resistance to all his native devils'."

In recent English Christianity there has been too much hard beating of the moral drum, too much exhortation to pursue high ideals—of disinterestedness, brotherhood, service, and so on. It has ignored that these aims are the fruit of a long historical religious tradition, which touched much more than the impelling of moral effort. This has perhaps a great deal to do with the widespread psychic breakdowns and anxiety states of our period. For pressure to reach certain standards of conduct without backing by forces in the soul or the culture of the epoch, puts an overwhelming strain upon the inner life of man. Hence the trend towards permissiveness all round in order to relieve the tension. The well-known passage in St. Paul's seventh and eighth chapters of his epistle to the Romans should have made clear beyond a doubt that the specific resources of Christian faith are not to be found in its inculcation of great moral ideals. Other faiths have nearly as good, and contemporary man has more ideals than he can manage. The resources of Christianity are to be found precisely in dealing with the devastating split between men's good aims and the more hidden forces, which mould the soul at a deeper level than that of conscious moral choice and clear eyed reason. St. Paul did not need the faith to give him good aims; he had these already. For him, the solution came not by harder willing or higher aims, but by discovering an outside power, which took possession and resolved the division of his inner life. He calls it the law of the spirit of life in Christ Jesus. In the same vein the Psalmist had exclaimed: "I will run the way of thy commandments when thou hast set my heart at liberty".

We are all of us familiar with the wretched situation, in which we have decided to act in a particular way, and then in a moment we find ourselves behaving in a quite opposite manner. Forces, of which we were unaware or thought we had mastered, have taken control. Our aims were not a growth out of the whole culture of the soul, but a kind of pressure from the top. A similar predicament affects society; the aims of its members are no good alone. Unless they are supported by the general habit of life and emotional patterns, the aims will be defeated and there will be set up psychic and social conflict. The influences, which form a society, are not so much its prevalent ideals as the way, in which millions live and work, their feelings, attitudes, hopes, loves and hates, the images they dream or imbibe from advertisement, pictures and radio. Idealism usually makes a picture of human life quite unrelated to these things and supposed that aims alone are decisive. That is one of the reasons why history is not predictable; why, for instance, the twentieth century has not the kind of society the men of the nineteenth thought they were creating. They were on the whole in the humanist liberal tradition and they believed they were merely giving men greater freedom and powers to embody that tradition. They looked upon their aims as furthering the expansion of the human personality. Why has that great aim faltered in the present century and been threatened by rival doctrines? Because it was, I think, a fine flower torn from its soil.

We could list a few of the aims in the recent humanist epoch such as: the disinterested pursuit of truth and learning independent of social pressures; ideas of right and wrong, which were not merely inscriptions on the banners of sectional groups; respect for persons and small groups as such whether they were social assets or nuisances. We see that such aims are severely threatened by totalitarian philosophies and régimes. We see, but less clearly, that they are in danger within the democracies too and we are inclined to think it is because they are weakly held. But we would be in a better position to understand the danger and possibly cope with it, if we realised that there are a number of influences in our industrialised culture, with its commodity hedonism, its standardised work and recreation, its technical incontinence, its anonymous ownerships, which tell against the aims and which we do not suspect of undermining them. A very central conflict between aims and cultures is that between the feeling tone induced by faith that each man and each creature has its ultimate significance from its relation to God, and then derivatively to others and to the world process. Twentieth century man is cajoled into feeling that he matters only as an item in world history; then of course he has no claims to significance other than that of being a citizen, a race-bearer, an economic producer or a human sink for products. You would not thank me for elaborating any further

the forces, which are moulding our culture and are threatening the aims derived from the classical Christian, humanist tradition.

This is not the place to propose remedies in the public sphere, but to point
out that society presents us with the same kind of task, which the Christian
believer finds in his moral quest. He knows that good aims are not enough and
that he cannot become "the new man" by sprinkling a little holy water upon his
deracinated willing. The Christian pilgrim learns to live in the appropriate climate, to immerse himself in the spiritual culture of the Church, however desic-
cated that may have become. This involves, at the immediate level, participat-
ing in the regular liturgical life of the Christian body, with its own cycle of the
Christian year, which does not coincide quite with the civil calendar or the
turns of the seasons. At a deeper level it involves experiencing with the corporate body of Christians that other movement—beyond the cycles of nature and
the irreversible movement of history—which cuts across them by a dimension
indicated in the terms, creation, redemption, and eternal life. In this dimension
the believer is incorporated with his fellows in the drama of Christ and the
word of God made flesh and the bearer of God's creative and re-creative power.
In addition, the Christian finds his own way to the reality of God behind the
flux of existence, in the depths of the soul, and learns by faith, prayer and discipline to live in the world with resources not derived from it. In all these ways
he is the partaker of an alternative culture, which fosters him in the commerce
he has with his secular commitments. His virtues become the fruits of the tree
rooted in Christ, the creative and renewing agent in all things. And with this
rootedness he can live and act with love and power in the rough and tumble of
the world without trusting it overmuch, for the world is then the place where
he puts forth his branches and fruit because he does not have his roots therein.

11. The Sphere of Knowledge

"I am persuaded of you, my brethren,
that ye also are full of goodness, filled with all knowledge,
able to admonish one another".
(Romans xv.14)

THIS IS ONE of the many places in the Scriptures where you will find goodness and knowledge mentioned side by side as if they were almost the same thing. Here St. Paul is counselling members of the Christian community in Rome not to bicker and quarrel, but to support one another, so that when some have to be corrected it will be clearly done by the kind of charity, which will be welcomed, and not resented by the vanity of the human soul. The goodness required for thus living as brethren we understand, whether we practise it or not; but why "knowledge"? What has that to do with brotherhood in Christ, or love to the neighbour? We could answer with the obvious remark that a man must know his neighbour's real needs—as distinct from his deluded wants and from what advisers tell him he needs. But more is at stake than that because the word used for knowledge is *gnosis*, the same term as that denoting the activity of the mind in becoming acquainted with *things*, with *subjects* and with *God*.

The fact is that *knowledge*, as used in the Bible, and, so far as I know, in all the great religious traditions, was never a purely mental grasp of something; it was an ability to do good or to experience good and evil. From the Genesis account of Adam's disobedience bringing about the first experience of the moral conflict, where that result is called "eating of the fruit of the tree of knowledge of good and evil"—to the statement in St. John "Ye shall know the truth, and the truth shall make you free"; knowledge is not a purely intellectual apprehending—but the ability to judge and act rightly. Some philosophers today have reminded us again—though it is ancient wisdom—of the difference between knowing that "such a thing is so"; and knowing "how" to do this or that. Other languages than English have two different words for these things—but the old Scottish word *ken*, for to "know" shows its link with "can", to be able.

That is the force of "knowledge" in the language of the Bible. What our translation renders, in this text of St. Paul "I am persuaded that ye are full of goodness, filled with all knowledge, able also to admonish one another" is rendered by a modern translator: "I feel certain that ye have a real Christian character and experience and that ye are capable of keeping one another on the right road". The word "experience" will do pretty well up to a point instead of knowledge—for "knowing how"—something for example which a young naval officer fresh from his technical college has to learn in the engine room of a battleship from the man who has lived with the machines for years but has had no theoretical training. That is experience of knowing how. But mere experience, however extensive, does not by itself bring ability to judge or to do things well. A man may be as old as Methuselah and be a fool, if he has learnt no principles of discrimination in order to sort out and evaluate his experiences. Maps are certainly no substitute for a holiday in Greece, but experience of that fair land will be the better for one who has looked at a map.

In the Scriptures, then, knowledge describes the kind of practical experience required to do things well; and when knowledge is used in the New Testament it carries with it the idea that this ability sprang from hearing God's word in Jesus Christ and relying upon his saving power; it is a recognition of the acts of God, in which the Christian participates; so knowledge of God is more than mental understanding, it is a new power, a sharing in Christ's achievements, which is involved in conversion to the Christian Faith. Lack of this kind of knowledge is therefore an offence as well as a mistake—a lack of obedience and of faith. But it has to be added that the *know how* of the Christian life, which is the same as knowing God, is not a withdrawal from the earthly historic scene, but the experience of the power of Christ resurrection and fellowship of His sufferings in the midst of our historical existence.

Now, someone who knows the Greek thinkers might quite well say to me: Is not what you are telling us about the Bible, that knowledge is a kind of practical goodness—is that not very much what Socrates taught and compressed into the saying "virtue is knowledge". The answer is "Yes", when you understand that for Greeks and Hebrews and Early Christians "knowledge" was not what it mostly means for us, just head knowledge, but the practical art of living. Indeed the Greeks have wrongly been understood to mean that the more you know in your head the better able you will be to manage your life, or that evil is due to ignorance of what is so. The answer to that misunderstanding of Socrates and Plato has been definitely given by Mr. John Gould in his book on Plato's Ethics [J.P.A. Gould, *The Development of Plato's Ethics*, Cambridge 1955]. There is no contradiction; both Bible and Greeks, when they said knowledge, they meant a habit of excellence, which had become a kind of skill through exercise. Of course, there are differences in the resources, from which Greeks and Hebrews draw their moral abilities.

Our difficulty today in grasping this wisdom, which linked knowledge and goodness so closely, is due to the fact that we are the heirs of a highly specialised piece of culture in our Western world—where knowledge has meant acquaintance with subjects: literature, history, science and so on. That part of our heritage has as a fact come out of the tradition of learning first born in Europe in the mediaeval monasteries, and then transferred to the world outside. But in addition we have inherited from the last two centuries a belief that increased knowledge of subjects would equip men better for a life worth living. It was due to a supreme act of faith (and has now become a mythology) that mankind was advancing morally by some process of social and mental evolution; its moral growth was a matter of time, emancipation and irreversible development. This faith fastened on Bacon's maxim "knowledge is power" and applied it in the sense that the more people know the quicker will they advance on the road to the good life. That faith has been rudely shaken among the discerning, though like all mythologies it is hardly at all upset by evidence to the contrary in the minds of its devotees. Many of us engaged in what we are pleased to call learning know that a multiplicity of information may not make for power but confuses our purposes and our judgment. The matter is made worse when we are subject to a battery of information, second-hand experience, impressions and exhortations from the press, the radio and the advertisers. Knowledge of this sort does not make for power, but diminishes it. We are afraid we might miss something. So don't believe everything you think you've been told.

Then we have been informed that knowledge in our modern sense makes for happiness. Well, yes, it does when it leads to a sort of initiation into a new world—that of the historian, the poet or the natural scientist—but this happens only when we are not tied to passing tests. Many are the definitions of education. One I remember was this: "It's like banging your head on a brick wall until you find a loose brick and get your head through". When we can forget the purely useful side of our pursuit of knowledge we may discover it as bringing us some kind of revelation admitting us to a new dimension. And that is a real happiness. But there is the other side: knowledge of life is knowing of sorrow as well as joy—Byron cried "sorrow is knowledge, and they who know the most must mourn the deepest o'er the fatal truth".

What I mean to lead up to is this. Knowledge of subjects such as a university rightly exists to foster will not by itself bring to us the skill of living the good and satisfying life. It can be part of it; but only if we have our spiritual and moral guidance from elsewhere. Otherwise, we will be missing the common source of our dreams and our science, like the character meditating in Eton College Chapel described in Aldous Huxley's *Antic Hay*: "No, but seriously, Gumbril reminded himself, the problem was very troublesome indeed. God as a sense of warmth about the heart, God as exultation, God as tears in the eyes, God as a rush of power or thought—that was all right. But God as truth, God as $2 + 2 = 4$, that wasn't so clearly all right. Was there any chance of their being the same?"

To pursue knowledge of subjects, secular as well as religious, as we are supposed to do in the university, can be vocation—something we are enabled to do and called to do because of our inheritance in a Christian culture, however far our subjects have got from the roots of education in the religious tradition. That early education in subjects—originally grammar, logic and rhetoric—was not undertaken to make people more godly—it was largely developed to make crude Christian princes, bishops and barons aware of the richness and variety of human experience, so that they could lead others well and not merely live by clashes of will and power. The good life, to which learning could minister, was given by other forces; namely by initiation in the Christian community and into another world, and that initiation brought the unveiling of a spiritual realm, in which men had their roots without knowing it until they learnt of it in the Divine Mysteries. Then they saw that the piercing of every barrier in knowledge was the same kind of revelation of a strange and wonderful new world, to which they before were blind.

12. Authority

"I am a man under authority having soldiers under me".
(Matthew viii.9)

AUTHORITY is a forbidding word, and the thing itself is much under fire today. Why should we obey the rules imposed by the moral tradition of the Church or by institutions like the state, the university, even the club? That is a common kind of question nowadays. Let us live, it is suggested, by our private judgement and our personal desires, unrestricted by authority of any kind, and we will find out by experience, by trial and error, pain and pleasure, what is right and wrong. That is the philosophy of life inculcated by many organs of public opinion. And even some Christian voices are running down authority in morals and advocating an untutored charity as the sole guide of life. That would be all right if all men were fully dedicated saints, but in a world of imperfect human beings some authority is inevitable, and everybody really knows that this is so. There is of course an inevitable resistance against any power, which is in the way of our self-will.

What people are mainly resisting when they decry authority is really something else, namely power imposing restrictions, which seem arbitrary, senseless or just tyrannical; and it often is. At one stage what is demanded cannot be authorised. "Why can't I do this, mummy?" gets the answer "because I say so". With the very young this often has to be said. But the day comes when the young thing will cease to obey and may even revolt unless it detects behind the order a reason, or has learned a confidence that in most things "mother really does know best"; and best in the sense of what effectively benefits those under orders. In other words, authority is power responsible to a truth, an order of things or a way of life, behind the person or institution, which exercises power.

We have in the Gospel of St. Matthew a concrete illustration. A non-commissioned officer, in charge of a hundred soldiers, asked Jesus to heal his epileptic servant. He adds immediately, don't trouble to come, just say the word.

I know what authority means, and therefore I discern that you have power over the created world, and can without your physical presence and touch set going the healing powers of the universe upon my suffering servant. Even if I am taking too much liberty in thus paraphrasing the scripture, notice how in the gospel's own language, this centurion justifies his confidence in our Lord's power. He says: "I am a man under authority", but goes on to explain, not who it is that is over him, but that he has people under him who obey his orders. "I say to this man go and he goeth, and to another come and he cometh, and to my servant do this and he doeth it". Our Lord performed the healing, but He said first this Roman soldier has more faith than all the Jews of Israel. The point he emphasised is that because he was under authority he could exercise it himself over subordinates. He did not mention the authority he served. It was in fact the Roman emperor during the reign of the puppet king Herod. In spite of cruelties and harshness the Roman Empire did exercise a rough justice throughout its far-flung provinces. That was why St. Paul could appear to Caesar and be protected on his way to Rome, when he claimed that the local powers were not true authorities but were acting arbitrarily. He went to the supreme political authority on earth.

We may say that authority is accredited power, power responsible to something above itself, which is recognized as being just. Human beings are pretty quick in sensing when power is wielded without authority. Men will ask, what right have you to command this? Children detect when parents have no way of life to guide them and to impart, and just impose their will. Pupils at school know when discipline is maintained for order and harmony's sake, and even when they catch it unfairly it's probably because teacher has got a bad headache. Students cannot help seeing whether a university teacher is acting, as it were, under the authority of his subject, or whether he or she is using their expertise as a personal advertisement, or their position as a warrant for domination.

When the Galileans who had heard the Sermon on the Mount marvelled at Christ's teaching we are told it was because He taught as one having authority and not as the scribes. Can we understand this as saying, He was lost in the truth He was declaring, not making a bid for recognition of Himself or showing His power. There was another occasion, recorded in the tenth chapter of Luke, when He said to the seventy disciples after they had gone around casting evil spirits out of many, and came back pleased saying "Lord, the devils are subject unto us", "Behold I have given you authority over all the powers of the enemy. Howbeit, in this rejoice not that the spirits are subject unto you; but rejoice that your names are written in heaven". Is not this to say: yes, the healing of men's souls is a good work; it has my authority; but the satisfaction must not be in your success, but in the integrity, which comes from doing the Lord's will, the pure intention, which makes a mark on the eternal slate.

From this principle that power is valid and has legality only when it has authority, that is, when it is responsible to a law above itself, which all men could recognize—from this principle several results have come, which are part of our Western civilisation. I will mention only two. First, there is our tradition of law. Our common law was controlled by the sense that the human ruler and legislator—king or parliament—was only entitled to obedience if he administered a justice, which he did not invent. The mere will of the sovereign did not make law. This was embodied in the famous formula *"Rex est sub deo et sub lege"*. It meant, in theory at any rate, that the ruling power was under the law as much as its subjects, and the subject had the right of disobedience if it were clear that power was used against the higher law. I said "in theory" because of course there have been countless acts of coercion with no authority. Rebellion has often followed sustained exercise of power without lawful authority. One feature of this aspect of authority is that, in this country, the judges are not part of the government, but independent representatives of justice.

The second application of the principle of authority, woven into the thought of Western culture, is the idea that lawful authority exercised by institutions and superiors, has responsibility to the nature of things. Members in a team of scientific researchers are loyal to their enterprise, without a boss giving orders, because there is an authority inherent in the job, to which they are committed. The craftsman, the architect, the city planner, the orchestral conductor, all have to rely in the end upon a diffused obedience to the task in hand and to the nature of the material used. On a wider scale, the power of institutions rests upon the nature of the things and beings they exist to deal with. One aspect of this doctrine that authority is rooted in the nature of things is illustrated by some words of the late Professor Arthur Eddington, the Cambridge scientist, in his book *The Philosophy of Physical Science*. Assuming the university customs of his day, he wrote:

"A stranger to our university, observing the undergraduates were inside their college walls before midnight, might believe that he had discovered a law of human nature—that there is something in the nature of the undergraduate, which impels him to seek the protection of the college walls before the stroke of twelve. We must undeceive him, and point out that the law has a quite different source—the college authorities. Should he conclude then that the law is altogether independent of undergraduate nature? Not necessarily. Careful research would reveal that the law depends on considerable antecedent experience of undergraduate nature. We cannot say that the twelve o'clock rule is not based on undergraduate nature; but it is not based on it in the way the stranger assumed".

We should perhaps have to add that the commandment of the college authorities rests not only on an estimate of undergraduate propensities, but also more fundamentally upon the nature of authority as a means of contributing to the fulfilment of the human lives they are temporarily charged with the care of.

To return, in conclusion, to the scriptures, the centurion recognized our Lord's power. If he had possessed a time machine and could have seen into the future he would have found theological support for that faith of his, in the Epistle to the Colossians, which declares Christ to be the power, in which all things consist. What Christ is and does and says discloses the nature of things, which is obscured to us because of our separation from God and from our own true nature. People often ask nowadays what authority has the moral teaching of the Church, and are frequently in rebellion against it. If one asks, why should I be meek, chaste, honest, why should I uphold the rights of others, why should I renounce the hold of worldliness upon me, the only convincing answer is not to say "the Church says so", but to bring the enquirer to see that what Christ asks of men is not to endure an uncomfortable straitjacket, but to accept His offer to re-create their true nature, which has been deflected. This means that the revealed moral law as given by our Lord has His authority because in it He voices the true nature of things, of which we have lost direct experience. It has to be shown to us, that is, revealed. This is a piece of religious teaching not much expounded today.

One of the most telling expressions of it was given by Richard Hooker, the Anglican divine of the sixteenth century, in Book One of his *Ecclesiastical Polity*. He wrote about the law of our nature, which is obscured by men's sinfulness, and there is therefore required a declared law, such as we have in the Commandments, the Sermon on the Mount and the moral teaching of the Church. "Nature is so spoiled, that though the sovereign good would be desired naturally, its fulfilment by natural means is made impossible by the fall. So we are by God's grace given the divine revealed law 'to rectify obliquity withal', to teach that what should be desired naturally must now be supernaturally attained". In one sentence, the commandments of Christ have the authority of Him by whom all things were made; and the supernatural life He imparts to His members restores human life to its true constitution. That is our Christian faith.

13. Permanence and Change

"Thus saith the Lord, Stand ye in the way and see,
and ask for the old paths, where is the good way, and walk therein,
and ye shall find rest for your souls". (Jeremiah vi.16)
"Be ye transformed by the renewing of your mind,
that ye may discern what is that good and acceptable
and perfect will of God". (Romans xii.2)

DO THESE two statements contradict one another? Jeremiah bids the people to return to the old paths. St. Paul tells his converts in Rome to become changed men by renewing their minds. Let us see. The career of Jeremiah marks the greatest crisis in the history of Hebrew religion, when the whole circle of beliefs and customs, which was centred in the Holy City and Temple, was suddenly broken by the destruction of Jerusalem at the hands of the invader from the north-east. Traditional faith could hardly have sustained a more staggering shock. The people had broken the covenant and Jehovah could no longer fulfil His promise to preserve the throne of David. Jeremiah was compelled to maintain the uselessness of resistance and was therefore, as he tells us, "in derision all the day long". But be cannot hold his peace. He is against the false prophets who assert that the Temple of the Lord is safe, and therefore all will be well. He knew with an aching heart that the conventional setting of religion was destroyed, but he did not say be would no longer trust the Lord for allowing it. True, his faith wavered at times, but it never broke, right up until his death among a handful of despised refugees in a foreign land where he had been forcibly taken. He faced facts, as we would say; the false prophets said he was dreaming. He answered that it was they who were living in a dream world.

I have chosen this piece of Bible history for, it seems to me, Jeremiah grasped so firmly that in the collapse of what was outward and secondary there could be found a way to what was essential and abiding. He knew what had to be given up because he knew what must be kept or recovered, and he was prepared to face a distasteful change in order that what was of changeless value might be attained.

And now for St. Paul; he urged upon the newly converted Christians in Rome the need for renewing their minds in order that they might learn God's will for them, and God's will is always for the fulfilment of the lives of His creatures. It must be remembered that for St. Paul "the mind" to be renewed is the whole inner life and not just the thinking part of us. It includes the will and the emotions, the purposes, and the deep mystery of the self, which in Christians is open to the unfathomable movements of the Holy Ghost. With such guidance as we can get from Jeremiah and St. Paul we may consider the problem every person and age and Church has to face, namely the question what has to be changed and what must be preserved as permanent or recovered if lost.

One of the dreariest clichés of the press, and often of the pulpit, is that we live today in a period of rapid social change. Those who use that phrase are sure that they are stating a fact; but listening more closely we find that they are persuading us to adapt ourselves to the changes going on. It is an example of what the philosophers call hiding an imperative in the guise of an indicative statement. It is a kind of salesmanship looking like enlightened observation. It persuades: you must have the latest thing, and soon after you will have to get another, for it is not meant to last and you cannot get it repaired! But it is not all salesmanship; there is also a theory that if things are not changing quickly mankind is stagnating or unprogressive. All this is called the idea of a dynamic society. But neither change or rapidity is of any value in itself, though we are being indoctrinated with that dogma. The most dynamic creatures in Holy Writ are the pigs running down the Gadarene slope. On the other hand I may at any time be grateful for the dynamic speed of an ambulance, or the swiftness of a rescuer's assistance. But if everything in life is in flux, nothing is worthwhile except for those who make money or get work from the world's incessant activity.

Can we get a little nearer to the heart of this problem? John Henry Newman said in his *Apologia*: "To live is to change and to live long is to change often". It means to change your direction if you have taken the wrong turn at the cross-roads or find your way blocked. It does not mean merely to change your speed. It implies, for instance, that if you have tried to handle life by your emotions only, you should cultivate the thinking part of you, and if you have tried to build your friendships and love life on reason only, you must turn and develop your feeling capacities. Such changes of direction may often require you to cultivate your weaker side, for if you devote all your energies solely to strengthen what you are good at, you may become an unbalanced monstrosity very difficult to live with. Furthermore, adaptation is change, but there are two kinds of adaptation necessary in life, and they are of opposite kinds. In one we have to adapt ourselves to new facts that cannot be altered or to situations we have wanted to bring about without realising all they imply. When a man gets married he must adapt himself to that situation and not behave as if he were still a dependent child. If you get a weak heart you can live long and well by practising a gentle rhythm of life. These are adaptations to desired or inevitable situations.

But another kind of adaptation is called for when you discover that certain developments need counteracting, because, though they may have been beneficial in one way, they have unbalanced life as a whole. For example, serious thought requires a certain amount of solitude and quiet; but it is strange what queer and crazy ideas a man can get if he never mixes with others of different interests or never hammers out his thoughts with his peers. When be discovers this he will adapt himself by balancing his solitude with social intercourse. Here is another case from the economic life: a society may go in for one main kind of product or crop only, because of quick gains in trade, and find that soon its economy is lop-sided and will cease to be humanly profitable. Adaptation then requires a variety or rotation of products. Or again, if you begin to suffer from some kind of rheumatism and then adapt yourself by following the inclination to stop moving your joints that will increase the danger of permanent immobility. The proper adaptation would be a kind of resistance. In all these examples, the first kind we may call wise adaptation to change; the second a wise adaptation towards normality or health, or the good life. It should be clear that if you practise the first kind when the second is needed, you are heading for disaster.

Change of direction, which is a necessary part of life, and certainly of its improvement, assumes that there is a central body of truth about our existence, which we by-pass or miss, or run away from. To reach it is a work of strategy where you change your plan in order to achieve your purpose. If I am playing chess my goal is to checkmate my opponent, but if I made a fixed plan before making my first move and did not change it according to the other player's moves, there would be no game. A general in war has the fixed aim of defeating the enemy, but he would soon be replaced if his every order were settled at the start. In brief, an unchanging goal requires a constantly changing plan of action.

It is not a new problem. St. Augustine wrote letters of advice to many who asked for guidance in that awful period when the Roman Empire was on its last legs; not long before he penned his last words the Vandal invaders were striking at the gates of his see city in North Africa. In one of his letters (No. 138 to one Marcellinus) he dealt with the enquiry how God who is unchangeable could accept the Old Testament sacrifices and then, when Christ had come, order their discontinuance. His answer is given in homely terms. The *paeda-gogus* or tutor gives to the adult youth different tasks from those, which he was accustomed to prescribe for the scholar in his boyhood. The teaching, consistent throughout, changes the instruction without the teaching changing in purpose. And the physician who prescribes for an illness is not surprised when a patient complains that the medicine he ordered ten years before was now useless or even harmful. The same man so much older is not the one for whom the pills were ordered. Thus the healing art in order to remain consistent in its aim must adapt its means to the moving circumstances of life. Trivial examples and obvious perhaps! But Augustine's point is often overlooked. There has to be a permanent aim or norm for changing adaptation to be beneficial. And now allow me an example from something said to me by Miss Dorothy Sayers shortly before she died. "People ask me", she said, "why I have stopped writing detective stories and entertaining them with the exploits of Peter Wimsey, and taken to religious drama and theological discussion and translating Dante instead. You must have utterly changed, they exclaim. I answer them, I have not really changed; you see, theology, learning to know God and the things of God is the most enthralling detective story of all".

That has my main point in a personal form: a permanent concern requires varying tactics, in order to hold on to it or to recover it. I think the mental and spiritual and material health of modern society is in danger of being lost because spokesmen of our public life are persuading a bewildered generation that there is no firm centre anywhere; they urge us to be dynamic all through, no matter whether the movement is in the genuine human interest or not. It too often comes to advocating a bigger dose of the same trouble when it is really an antidote that is needed, or saying that if you find yourself in a mess you had better get messier in order to suit it. That is what is meant by "progress", so often mistaken for improvement, going faster along the same old grooves when it is a change of direction that is called for.

Our Christian faith has its own unchanging convictions. They concern the nature of God, of His world, of His saving acts and our response. This is enshrined in our creeds; but these are only the skeleton of our living worship and understanding. In order to keep this unchanging faith alive there may be required change in Church organisation, in forms of service, in the language of our religion. But the content of our faith is constant, and the Church has always got to look out lest by changing its language and its form in order to meet the mentality of today, the faith itself and not just its expression is changed, becoming another religion with the same name. Arthur Hugh Clough wrote these well-known lines:

> "Old things need not be therefore true,
> o brother man, nor yet the new;
> Ah! still awhile the old thought retain
> And yet consider it again".

In order to be adaptable the human being needs an abiding point of certainty and settlement, a rock of ages, an anchor of the soul, and be able to sing with confidence "O Thou that changest not, abide with me". Jeremiah and St. Paul knew this need and called on their listeners to change their hearts in order to learn it.

14. The Grace of Humility

"I say to every man, not to think of himself
more highly than be ought to think,
but to think soberly (with no illusions)".
(Romans xii.3)

WHEN William Master arranged that at his death in 1684 there should be endowed out of his estate two annual sermons to be preached in this University, by the titles he designed for them he seems to have displayed an insight into the subtleties of the human heart, which can be found exhibited in the one publication of his own, *Essays and Observations Theological and Moral, Wherein Many of the Humours and Diseases of the Age Are Discovered*, a work, which bears comparison with *The Anatomy of Melancholy* by Robert Burton, half a century his senior. William Master designed his two endowed sermons to be entitled, one on *The Sin of Pride,* the other on *The Grace of Humility.* It is this latter, which is assigned to me today; and when I find that *Humility* is described as a grace, where we might expect it to be called a virtue, making a clear contrast to *Pride,* which is called a sin, I begin to see why it is more difficult to discourse about *Humility* than about *Pride.*

For one thing, the more one talks about humility, the greater the temptation to think of it as a virtue, which the speaker represents and which then easily becomes the material of a disguised kind of pride. Then, also, there are no dramatic myths about humility as there are about *ubris* or pride, like the fall of Lucifer or the fate of Prometheus. Further, an exposition of humility cannot be so interesting as the piquant pictures of human pretentiousness to be found in the moral satirists such as Juvenal, La Bruyère or Bernard Mandeville with his characteristic oracular statement that "the nearer we search human nature, the more we shall be convinced that the Moral Virtues are the Political offspring which Flattery begat upon Pride" (*Enquiry into the Origin of Moral Virtue* in *The Fable of the Bees* [1714]). Such are the difficulties in making *humility* interesting; and they account for the common tendency to expound it by contrast with the more enthralling displays of human self-exaltation—and perhaps also for the glee, with which the eighteenth-century moralists disclosed how easily self-conscious humility becomes a subtle form of self-esteem. But this had been a commonplace among the Christian spiritual writers.

I think it therefore probable that William Master was aware of this common self-deception when he did not put humility under the heading of a virtue but under that of a grace, something in the nature of a gift, which cannot be acquired by effort. If I am right in this surmise, then William Master would be a precursor of Coleridge, who in *Aids to Reflection* declared: "we will value humility the more, yea, then only will we allow it true spiritual worth, when we possess it as a gift of grace, a boon of mercy undeserved, a fulfilment of a free promise". And nearer to our own time I find the great Oxford divine of this century Hastings Rashdall saying: "the good man will ascribe his goodness to 'grace', recognising that his good qualities are due in the first instance to parentage, influence, example, social tradition, education, community, Church, and ultimately, if he is a religious man, to God". And one could find right through the history of Christian spirituality the enigmatic place accorded to humility. "There is no single activity, which could be called humble, it is rather a quality, which flavours what a man does. Humility is given to men obliquely; it is, as it were, a by-product of a religious style of living". St. Thomas Aquinas put it down as a quality of charity and magnanimity; and he was surprisingly free from certain medieval tendencies to encourage excessive self-abasement. Humility is not listed in the old manuals under the virtues. More surprisingly it is not included among the fruits of the Spirit in St. Paul's Epistle to the Galatians: "love, joy, peace, long-suffering, goodness, faith, meekness, temperance", the main characteristics of the self in whom the Holy Ghost is working. But humility is tacitly enjoined over and over again by Christ and the Apostolic writers, not as a separate virtue, but as a quality, which must penetrate the practice of all the others. Nor is it one of the crowning fruits of the Christian life, like love, zeal, courage, and joy, but a kind of foundation temper, which opens the closed oyster of the self.

Anyone acquainted with the pre-Christian moralists, who might read for themselves the words of St. Paul, which I have chosen as the text, "I say to every man, not to think of himself more highly than he ought to think"—such a reader might well say, this is of no help at all; how do we know how we ought to think of ourselves, and if we try to work it out are we not turning inwards and concentrating on the self, taking its moral pulse, all of which prevents the kind of loss of self, which makes the truly humble person. Or they might say, even if St. Paul's dictum is a real guide, the injunction contains no more than what Socrates or Aristotle taught. And indeed that is true, so far as the words go. Aristotle had called a man modest "who estimates himself justly", that is to say, accurately. But though St. Paul uses the same kind of language, suggesting that humility is a kind of truthful self-knowledge, he follows this precept with the passage about the diversity of gifts. All have not the same powers of functions, just as parts of the body have not the same office in the body. Some offices or functions are more exalted than others, but whether a man be a prophet, or a servant, or a teacher, or a leader, each is equally valuable in performing this one of unequal tasks. So none may glory in a more exalted function, nor feel inferior in a more lowly one. In this kind of "proportionate equality", which is the mark of members in the Christian family, to lack humility is not so much to be in ignorance of one's true character, but is rather a moral failure, especially a failure in liberality or love, or a failure to accept without envy or arrogance the work God gives to each one.

We might translate St. Paul's words in this way. Do not cherish a flatteringly false picture of yourself; learn to see what you really are without intoxicating or somnambulist illusions. Even if we leave out the whole Christian context of the passage, and look at it as the Greeks would do, it is still a pretty tall order. How are we to know what we really are? Augustine said it was easier to know God than to know oneself. He knew that we could only form a true estimate of that, if we have a standard of measurement outside ourselves, which is completely above bias and illusion. For Augustine that was the mind of God as disclosed in His Word, Jesus Christ Our Lord. To see as God sees is to see things as they really are. But even without this specifically Christian account of the matter, there is a lot in literature, which recognises that the self of everyday life and the self as the self sees itself is not the authentic self. This question preoccupied men like Thomas Carlyle and Leo Tolstoy. In everyday life each of us is in some way invariably an actor; we live up to a pattern, which will get us along, and if we act our part too thoroughly it becomes harder to distinguish our theatrical ego from the real one. Perhaps the need to be free of the counterfeit self is the meaning of our Lord's injunction to the disciple to become as a little child; so young that it has not yet begun to pose at all. Men and women have often fled to solitude in order to strip themselves of the disguising garments, with which they feel they have distorted their authentic selves—and a great deal of the spiritual discipline of Christendom and of the Eastern religions has had the same aim.

No Christian writer has been harder on the counterfeit self than Pascal. He said, self is hateful. It is unjust in itself because it makes itself the centre of all things, and it is disagreeable to others, because it would bring them all into subjection! In another of his *Pensées* he remarks that we are forever seeking to adorn and maintain our imaginary self, and we neglect the true one. Now, the stripping of the false self in order to become the authentic self is the very essence of all the great religious traditions of mankind; it has badly been lost sight of in our modern Western culture, even in the religious part of it, which has become concentrated upon what men do in and to the world. And this neglect has its revenge in movements for strange kinds of regeneration, and refuges from our habits of intensive activism. I have in mind the search for inner poise, for which people are looking to a foreign kind of Yoga, or efforts by means of drugs to save the soul from the pain of incessant demands upon the self to be doing, when the selves have lost awareness of their own validity. I think also that this teaching of the recovery of the authentic self is a better clue to the meaning of humility than arithmetic calculating good or bad points in a person's character; certainly better than comparison between oneself and others.

Humility is not much admired today. It suggests a passive attitude to things, subservience to the powers that be; and a hindrance to the relentless conquest of nature that for *Homo Faber*, the tool-devising animal, has come to be thought the most significant aspect of human existence. Doctrines about inner transformations are OUT, so far as modern man's dominant interests are concerned. The self, just as it is and as it acts, is taken for granted, and in fact unconsciously it has become the centre of all things. This process has quite a history by now; it largely stems from the result of the Copernican revolution when at the same time the astronomers and scientists taught us that man and his world are not the centre of the universe, and the philosophers set about to show that mentally he is the centre. Thought became concentrated upon the thinking and knowing process, rather than on the things to be apprehended. One recent result in morals is the absence in the minds of many people of any recognised standard outside themselves, by which to measure their character or behaviour. This absence is called relativity in morals—good and bad for this man or this group is just what each considers to be good or bad; Right and Wrong are no more than labels to indicate preferences; or they are banners proclaiming support for this or that group in the struggle for place in the general flux and conflict of existence. This mental atmosphere is the fruit of recent teaching that man is the centre of his own world. At its most extreme, there is no world at all. The world is the way we look; good and evil is the way we feel. In such a mental climate there is nothing we can check our illusions by, no pattern of goodness or greatness given to us to be humble in the presence of, and certainly no heroes to admire.

A second way, in which humility is neglected or misunderstood, is a failure to distinguish between the quality of a man and that of his work. A work may be good—in science, art or literature, in building, fabricating and so on but the doer of that good work is not thereby a good person. Many a bad man has produced good works. For instance, some of the most worldly and unscrupulous prelates of the Renaissance made fine appointments of saintly priests to Church positions. They had a good nose for sanctity and knew its value, although they themselves kept as far from its realisation as possible. Humility does not argue: my work is good therefore I am good.

Having said all this, I must add that of course there is a right kind of pride in good work; perhaps satisfaction would be a better term than pride, for this concern for excellence is not at all incompatible with humility. It only becomes the meat of pride, in the bad sense, when attention is shifted from the good of the work to the doer of it. To be less concerned with the good of the work than with the fact that it is I who am doing it—that is the loss of humility. To be puffed up because of qualities we do not possess but imagine we do, beauty, or brain power or statesmanship—is not pride; it is merely conceit. That is not sinful; it is merely a mistake. But to be puffed up because of what we can do, or qualities one really possesses, that is pride, the opposite of humility. And even so, some kinds of pride are not serious. It does a man no great harm to be proud of his ancestors, or of his country, or of his inheritance, his school or college, because he has done nothing to have them. As Lord Melbourne said of the Garter decoration, there is no damn merit in it. It is more harmful, and destructive of humility to be proud of having made money; and still more, to go up the scale, to be proud of one's intellect; and most disastrous of all to be proud of one's moral achievement. It is a Christian commonplace that the Saints do not know themselves as holy but consider themselves great sinners. St. Paul spoke of "sinners of whom I am chief". How could he say that? Had he compared himself with all other men, and then judged that they were all better than he? Of course not. He measured himself by what God had shown him he was intended to be. In that light he was the only sinner with whom he was concerned. So he was anxious lest having preached to others he should be himself a castaway.

Humility is concerned with the thing done; not with the doing of it by men. Here the difficulty is to get out of the way, and here is the catch about humility. If it is regarded as a virtue, instead of a grace, one can become unconscious of it, and that makes a grotesque caricature, like Dickens' Uriah Heep. I remember such a man. He was a sidesman and after the Vicar had preached on the text in the Psalm: "I would rather be a doorkeeper in the house of God than dwell in the tents of ungodliness", he said to the Vicar: "That was a wonderful sermon. I often think I would rather be even a doormat, than dwell haughtily in the tents of wickedness". When he had gone the Vicar remarked: "I guess a wet day would try him". When we are taken out of ourselves we are humble, immersed in what we are doing. And when we are pleased, too; for then we attend to what pleases us; when we are miserable it is on ourselves and not the cause that we concentrate. Lovers are humble, for each is wrapt up in the beloved; until they become concerned with love instead of the other one. Small children are humble for they ask questions because they want answers and are glad when they get them. But then all too soon the day arrives when the things to be known begin to take second place, and awareness of knowledge becomes a dominant interest, and one says to the other: "I know more than you". That is the fall away from humility. The primal image of the world recedes, and its place is taken by the secondary image of oneself as knowing. That is what grows into something the world of learning badly suffers from now; knowledge in the academic sense has become a status symbol.

There is a frightening picture, of this fall from concern with the thing to be known, to concern with knowing, in Charles Williams' novel, *Descent into Hell*. There Wentworth is a good historian, but he loses his first love of history, and transfers it to himself as historian. When a colleague is honoured, he is not pleased and does not even send congratulations. Very soon he begins to falsify his facts and writes to gain a reputation, and many suffer on the way. It is a descent into hell, this gazing of the self upon the self. Some have said that this is the meaning of Lilith in the Rabbinic literature—Lilith, the nocturnal spirit who was Adam's first wife, not a real woman out there like Eve, a true other, but Adam's picture of himself, his own desire answering his own desire. In magical lore she is called the Succubus and in Greek literature the Siren. She is also the statue Pygmalion made out of his own mind, fell in love with it, and it took the goddess Aphrodite to turn it into a real live woman. The legend does not say whether the goddess made Pygmalion's brain woman to be a real one, so that she might get him by the ear to dissipate his dream image. To return to our theme, humility is an escape from the squinting round upon the self, which is doing this or that; it is being immersed in the thing done or enjoyed. It is not to take a low view of oneself or of one's work. Supremely, for the Christian it is to be given over to what God and the world presents to us, and our response to them. Then we get as near as human nature can, to seeing as God sees, namely seeing things as they truly are.

I conclude with reflections of the greatest of all exponents of humility and pride, St. Bernard of Clairvaux. Besides a treatise on *Twelve Degrees of Humility and Pride*, he wrote a work called *De Diligendo Deo* on man's love for God. There he warns his readers not to think humility means to take a low view of human nature. He knows it is often a disguised form of pride to say: "I am such a poor creature; you cannot therefore expect too much of me". Such talk is to safeguard one from the humiliation of failure, and that fear is born of pride, not of humility. St. Bernard tells us to be aware of man's dignity—the exalted nature of being made in God's image, "by which", he says "it is given to man to excel, and to rule over all other creatures. Knowledge also is given to man, by which he knows this dignity to be in himself, but not from himself. It is necessary therefore to know what thou art (namely, this honourable nature) and that thou art not of thyself (for as St. Paul says, What hast thou that thou hast not received) lest thou glory not at all, or glory vainly".

15. A Difficult Text on Providence

"The very hairs of your head are all numbered".
(Matthew x.30)

THE HAIR of a person's head has been used in proverbial statements as a symbol of smallness, insignificance, un-uniqueness, in texture if not in length. "A hair's breadth" means the tiniest imaginable dimension. To sling a stone or shoot an arrow, as in the Book of Judges, to a hair's breadth is practically to hit the target. And when King Saul or Solomon wanted to assure a captive that he was quite safe from injury, how did they put it? "Not a hair of you shall fall to earth", which is to say, even the least essential part of you will be respected and protected. A hair, in these proverbial phrases, is the nearest physical symbol of nothingness. And in the romantic literature a hair, as flimsy as a spider's thread and more tenuous than a gossamer scarf, has been held as the image of something so little resistant that to cut in two a hair floating down the breeze with a sword, has been pictured as the most wonderful achievement of swordsmanship and of the tempering skill of the sword-maker; more wonderful than cleaving wood or rook. With regret I cannot interpret George Meredith's tantalizing allegory *The Shaving of Shagpat* where the single hair of Shagpat's otherwise bald head somehow stands for collective evil, which the reforming hero sets out to shave off, and has to encounter many trials and obstacles in order to get at it.

However, we find that a hair is the symbol of that created thing which to our physical eyes looks quite lacking in individual character, so like every other on the same head, and so inessential to the personality. But if you were to pluck a hair out by the root and look at it under a microscope you would see not just an elongated filament, but a complex organic structure with a little sac secreting oil, so that brushing the hair vigorously lubricates it and makes it shiny, as many a wise girl has discovered. What is more, a biologist who is an expert on hair,

I suppose a capilliarist we should call him, would detect separate characteristics of each specimen on a person's head, quite hidden from our ordinary sight.

All this does, I think, take us some way in grasping the force of our Lord's saying that even the hairs of each one's head are numbered, not only counted by God, but estimated each one as a valid significant bit of His creation. Is this a difficult text, telling us that God cares for the tiny as well as for the great whole of the created world? Well, yes, there are two difficulties. One is the general puzzle of our having to use physical space language to express spiritual facts. When we declare that God is infinite, not finite, it suggests to us that He attends only to the large and not to the small. But the infinity of God means exactly the opposite. He is spirit, and therefore the physically minute is as much His concern as the physically huge. "Beware", says the nameless author of *The Cloud of Unknowing*, "that you take not bodily what is meant ghostly". And the fourth century theologian, Nemesius of Emesa, speaks of God as "the unembodied nature penetrating everything without obstacle, but is itself impenetrable". This same Nemesius, not in the first rank of theologians but of considerable importance, wrote a treatise *On the Nature of Man* with a final section on *Divine Providence*. In that section he has an interesting comparison between Plato and Aristotle. He finds a paradox there. It was Plato, with his main interest in general and universal ideas, who sees God's providence upholding the small and the particular. Aristotle, on the other hand, stressed the individual and particular aspects of the world as the only realities, and because his god was impersonal, he could not see the divine hand as providentially caring for the individual and the singular.

This general difficulty of envisaging God's hand in the minute, due to our inadequate visual and spatial language, is sometimes removed in devotional expression. The sacramental hymn, the *Lauda Sion*, contains the words "Thousands are as one, receivers, one as thousands of believers, takes the food that cannot waste; whoso of this food partaketh, rendeth not the Lord nor breaketh". Each receives the whole Christ. He is as much in each part of the worshipping body as in the whole. Our spatial separateness and mutual exclusiveness are quite overcome at this level.

But now, in addition to the general difficulty for our intellects, there is an added stumbling block for many modern Christian minds who have been misled into losing the specifically biblical view of the relation of God to His world. The Bible has one ultimate premiss, the world's meaning cannot be found inside the world itself. And because the creator God transcends the world, each part has its meaning from that part's relation to the divine source, and not primarily from its place in the whole. That is why Christianity with its Bible sees the individual person and thing as having significance in itself and not merely because it is a co-operating item in a larger process, the state, the race, the nation, economics or the biological life of the world. The reality and significance of the individual is guaranteed because each creature is by its own unique specific accidents a participator in the divine action. When Newman said "religion has to do with the real and the real is always the particular" he was underlining that particular things, persons, communities and periods, behind their links with the rest of creation, have their singular value from the sustaining power of God. People today have largely lost this discernment because they have been deflected into believing only in a kind of general providence that may guide the whole but leaves the myriad detailed items to the forces of nature, history, mechanism or fate. Tennyson in the last century helped this error by seeing only the one far-off divine event, to which the whole creation moves, as if there are no divine actions short of the final consummation. And some aspects of "process" theology encourage the same departure from biblical insights, suggesting that the parts are only significant for the sake of the whole, or as steps leading up to a final enlightenment when it will be seen eventually that "It's all right on the Omega night".

There should be no serious difficulty for the Christian mind, which grasps this relation of God and the world as giving significance to the tiniest part of it. One sparrow is the concern of the Father, and sparrows are five for twopence in the market place. And the hairs of one's head are the objects of His providence. The serious perplexity of the passage is not in the text itself, but in the call of Christ to His followers to put away all anxiety for what happens to them. The word about God caring for hairs and sparrows is the reason given why the disciple can abandon himself to divine providence, even when in danger of being killed. In Matthew vi Jesus bids His disciples to behold the lilies and the birds who take no thought for the morrow. How are we to take that? No anxiety about the future, what clothes we put on or take off, what shall we eat or what is the state of our bank balance; or what shall we answer when questioned? Shall we not look at old examination papers before Schools? Shall we have no concern about what we shall do in the world? And if we are forbidden to plan and arrange, who is to fill the begging bowls and provide for one's children? Let us look at this challenge of Jesus straight in the face. The disciple must be prepared for persecution, suffering, scorn and so on, and not doubt God's hand in it. But how can one live as the lilies and the birds who have no anxiety, for they have no knowledge of the next day? We can note two things.

Our Lord is not forbidding forethought; He enjoined it. If you attend a marriage you must get a wedding garment; you must make sure you have the material before starting to build a house; you must ensure enough troops before you fight; you must see that your skin bottle has no holes in it before you pour in the wine; you must provide oil for your lamps if you go to meet the bridegroom. Here is a fine puzzle; we are to plan and find the necessary means, and yet we are to accept everything that happens as in the Lord's keeping, as providential! Intellectually Christians have never solved this puzzle. Men have tried to, and have often done so by positing two levels of divinity, one who is the upholder of all but unconcerned with each, another the gods and goddesses who are involved in men's affairs but are not supreme.

There is no intellectual resolution, but there is a practical one. Fully half of our anxieties and doubts of God's providence are due not to what happens to us or could, but to the problems of our disordered state. How to deal with these is too long a story to begin now. A hint must suffice. You know how much we are at the mercy of circumstances, the forces that invade our life from outside and throw doubt upon God's providential care. It is then that we can by grace and spiritual exercise rest our human spirit upon God and find that our innermost self is not shifted from its central place to go fussing around to resist the tiresome influences of the outside world. We discover what St. Theresa called "the interior castle", the deepest of the "many mansions" of our inner life. Of it she writes: "I shall think of our soul as of a castle formed of a single diamond or of a very bright crystal, in which there are many rooms, just as in heaven there are many mansions... some of these are above, others below, and others on either side, and in the centre, in the midst of them all, is the chiefest of them, where most secret things pass between God and the soul". Everyone has this innermost mansion in the interior castle of the soul. It is there the real self acts and knows the present of God. To be assured that this interior castle is not invaded or destroyed by the outer circumstances of our life is a condition of deliverance from false anxieties. I am not saying that you won't ever suffer, but the things you endure will not crush you, or make you timid, morose, touchy, grousy or resentful. All that uses up your inner powers like a badly oiled engine, which spends most of its energy in overcoming internal friction. Do not then let your faith in God's providence depend upon harmony in your soul. But disregard the scraping noises your private anxieties make, and by turning that innermost centre of you, your self, round to its source in God, you will reach some balance. What is left of disturbance and doubt will not matter. The frustrations that make us doubt God's providence, often the generous anxiety of how little we can do to lighten suffering in the great world, are great trials. But just when our mood says "if only things were different for me I could have confidence", just then our Lord calls for the faith, which acknowledges His providential care for even the single hair of your head.

16. Has Religion a Future?

"When the Son of Man cometh shall He find faith on earth?"
(Luke xviii.8)

S ON OF MAN", as the scholars will tell you, is one of the Bible terms for Messiah. In the imagery of Ezekiel, "son of man" is not a human being born of a woman, but of strange supernatural power from heaven, which had the likeness of a man. In this text from St. Luke's Gospel, Jesus identified himself with one of the Old Testament images of the saviour. So we may take His own question as asking will there be any religious faith at the end of the world, when history is over?

Those of us who retain some allegiance to the Christian Church, its faith and worship, may well wonder, when we face the fact that religious believers are a deviant minority, out of the main stream of modern thought and interest. But to hold convictions, which are not shared by the world at large, need not by itself be depressing for Christian believers. What does make things look black for the future of religion is the assumption, shared by all men of today, Christian, agnostic and atheist, that the future will be a continuation of the recent past and present. If they have same historical knowledge people can point to the changes in outlook from the seventeenth century, when a religious view of the world began to be replaced by what we call secular interpretations. These interpretations see the universe and man's place in it, as accounted for entirely in terms of the world process itself—without any reference to an eternal, divine reality, transcending the world while acting in and upon it; in another dimension, as it were. This dismissal of the supernatural has little to do with modern confidence in the scientific method and the great benefits it has brought about. I can only assert, without going into the whole story, that there is no conflict between natural science and religion. There is a conflict between the religious view of things and modern thought. Modern thought is secularist, but it is not based on science, though it often thinks it is. The unbelieving modern world is not composed of intellectuals who have looked at religious belief and rejected it. It is comprised of millions for whom the religious understanding of man, with its reference to a divine reality, has just ceased to have any meaning for men coping with the intellectual and practical problem of life. It does look as if the growth of religious belief is a continuing process, and that religion will die out, or it did so look perhaps until quite recently. We can trace some stages in the process. Before it started there was Roger Bacon in the thirteenth century, one of the Oxford Franciscans, who held that all knowledge was experimental, but this is of two kinds, experiment on external nature, the source of certainty in natural science, and experimental acquaintance with the work of the Holy Spirit within the soul, the source of the knowledge of heavenly things, which culminates in the vision of God.

Four centuries later Isaac Newton, himself a very religious man, tried to make a synthesis between his conception of the universe as a marvellous mechanism and his religious faith. He spent many hours and wrote many pages on this: but in the end he had to admit that a purely mechanical view of the world was incompatible with the older organic spiritual scheme of the universe. We don't quite know whether Newton regarded his physics and mathematics as just a science of the material world, and held that there were other levels of being. What is certain is that his followers thought of it as *the* science, the only legitimate knowledge of the objective world. Thereafter science and religion appeared to be totally divorced. Then in our own day, at least for the older ones of us, we have witnessed the whole picture of the universe as a self-regulating machine, broken up by Einstein and his theory of relativity. This has been considered to be a more open, fluid picture of the world. But a philosopher like Whitehead, when he was told he must not be so distressed because Newton's view of the world was in ruins and that he could find comfort in relativity, exclaimed: "No, thanks, I've been fooled once and I will not be fooled twice". And religious thinkers have thought that the abandonment of a mechanical universe left crannies for the perception of divine or supernatural interpretations. So instead of the world as a machine, they now talk of the world as a process. But that again is still a one-world view, with no opening to the religious up-and-down dimension of existence. It is still a closed world with no power of renewal from above or outside.

All this, however, is somewhat beside the point, when we are considering the future of belief and unbelief. Not by any means are all scientific workers irreligious; secularist attitudes are held by historians, sociologists, and philosophers. And religious unbelief is not confined to intellectuals whose thought appears to them to conflict with religious faith. To the vast majority it is not a question of credibility: "Can we believe what religions and the Church say?". No, their question is rather: "Does religion and the Church say anything that matters?", or: "Why should I try to find out what they say and do. It has nothing to do with me; let those who go in for religion do so. But it is not my world at all". There are, I think, two things to remember, which throw some light on this situation where the greater number of people in the modern world is alienated from the faith, thought and worship of the religious bodies. One is that ordinary people hate being thought odd, or belonging to a minority group, much as an artisan might say: "I could not go to work in a suit, they would think I was a manager or something". Unbelief spreads, as it becomes the attitude of majorities and fashionable. For men are pretty gregarious and conformist beings for the most part. The other thing to remember is that while the belief and practice of Christians is confined to a minority in our society, if we look at it historically, in terms of the career of mankind, unbelief or secularism in a large sense is a comparatively recent phenomenon, not three hundred years old. We now know that mankind has lived with religions for most of its history in primitive tribes, in the ancient civilisations and in seventeen hundred years of Western history. What then are we to make of this situation; conformity of unbelief in the human space of our day, and the non-conformity of unbelief in time? There are only two possible answers: either to say the modern world is too enlightened by now to take religion seriously, or on the other hand that our civilisation has given its members so many other preoccupations and interests that the facts, for which religion stands, have dropped out of consciousness. It has often been asked why in the nineteenth century what was called the working class was lost to the Churches; with the exceptions of the Methodist Revival and the Roman Catholic Church. Some have answered: the unbelief of the clever intellectuals has spread down to the industrial town and factory. Not a bit of it. The industrial population has not been through a crisis of belief, in fact it is not even now completely secularised. It uses Churches for baptisms, marriages and burials. As for the Church of England, Professor Brogan may be right when he said: "the Church of England is the Church the majority of English people stay away from, but they want it there to stay away from".

No, it is not that the mass of our fellow citizens have had a look at Christianity and rejected it. It is rather that the industrial revolution landed them with problems, becoming more complex every day, and the message of the Churches was not of any guidance to them. So their hopes, interests and preoccupations were directed elsewhere, to the secular world itself and the questions it presented to them. The language, imagery and belief of the Churches seemed not of any importance; it did not fit in anywhere in their purposes and thought, as it escaped from their awareness.

There is a frequently quoted illustration of this kind of absence of attention to things, which do not seem to affect people's concerns. It comes from Charles Darwin's account of his travels in the voyage of the Beagle. When that ship arrived in a bay at the tip of South America, they anchored the ship well outside and proceeded to the shore in small dinghies. The natives were so excited at the sight of small boats about the size of their own canoes that they tried to talk about nothing else. But they paid not the slightest attention to the schooner, lying, large as life, out there in the bay. This is a common situation. We are interested in novelties within the sphere of our own experience and expertise. The natives of Tierra del Fuego knew about small boats; they felt neither curiosity nor wonder concerning things like ships so far beyond their experience that they even had not a name for them. But the dinghies of the Europeans were so like their own canoes that their interest was aroused, as if they had discovered old friends in a new disguise. It would be wrong to say they did not believe in the large sailing ship. It was simply that it had no significance for them: it had no bearing upon what they were familiar with, and upon the things they did.

It is something like that, which has happened to our part of the human race. What looks like a decline of religion, is really a loss of certain kinds of insight and experience, and this means that the language of religion is not about anything most people are involved in. Can we have a description of what I have here too generally called religion? Well, here is the definition given by an outstanding student of religion, the philosopher and psychologist, William James—author at the beginning of this century of a book called *The Varieties of Religious Experience*. He wrote: "Religion consists of belief that there is an unseen order, and that our supreme good lies in harmoniously adjusting ourselves thereto". That is all right as far as it goes, but even if we are thinking of religions in general, we should have to add two other things: first, the rituals. Religion is not only belief, but acts such as prayer and worship and putting oneself in open attention towards the power of this unseen world. Secondly, this unseen world as William James called it, is a sacred realm, which calls out of the worshipper a sense of awe and reverence. This much is common to all religions. And at a time when Christians are thinking much about coming to an understanding of the faith of the Far East and Islam, too many of our Christian leaders want to drop out this element of the holy and sacred from their presentation of Christianity. But belief in a sacred realm and our proper attitude to it, is the common stuff of all the faiths, even those who have no personal God. The distinguishing mark of Christianity with its Bible, however, is that created beings have no sacredness in themselves; only the Lord is Holy. Persons, things, actions, acquire a sacredness as they are dedicated to the one Holy Lord, consecrated, as we say. And the Christian faith adds as its central affirmation that the divine holiness is not merely the quality of a distant God, but is embodied in the person and work of Jesus the Christ.

You will have noticed a shift back to some kind of religion. It comes not from those in the Church who tend to adapt their teaching to the mind of modern man; it comes instead from the revolt of youth who reject the secular aims of technological and commercial Western society. What if these movements and unconstructive and often unhealthy? They represent a search for spiritual modes of consciousness. They contain not only a confused medley of religious elements together with occult magical rubbish and drug experimentation; they also seek light from oriental forms of spiritual discipline and meditation. If the religious and sacred is kicked out of the front door, it will come in by the back door, with a lot of demons in its train.

IV. Social

17. Human Rights

"The Lord will not turn away the right of a man".
(Lamentations iii.55)

"THE RIGHTS OF MAN" is a phrase that has played a large part in our Western civilized history. It appears that over and over again men have to discover what rights human beings have in this world; and then there is a second question: what kind of society, with its customs and laws, is best able to ensure that men are accorded what they have a right to?

There have been many statements of the rights of man: political rights like those of Magna Carta; moral rights like the right to exist and not to have one's life taken away. Yet in spite of a long and varied history there is still need to formulate rights for the whole of mankind. What, we may ask, is implied in according to each man his due. You might think there have been enough of such declarations. The Pilgrim Fathers, when they were making their constitution for New England, laid down certain rights, which were to a large extent based on the Christian conception of human nature. The American Declaration of Independence began with these words: "We hold these truths to be self-evident, that all men are endowed by their Creator with certain inalienable rights, that among these are life, liberty and the pursuit of happiness". Then at the French Revolution human rights were more often regarded as something innate, belonging to man by nature, which could be discovered by the human reason without any religious foundation. And there have been repeated attempts since. A session of the Institute of International Law in 1929 declared that it is the duty of every state to recognize for every individual the equal right to life, liberty and property and to accord to everyone on its territory the full and complete protection of the law without distinction of nationality, sex, race, language or religion.

Today, fifty years later, it is realized that in the international world there are many sets of people who are deprived of elementary human rights either because they live under oppressive tyrannies, or they have no state responsible for them. This applies especially to "stateless" persons and refugees.

Now, concern for the rights of man is not something confined to Christendom. You can find rights laid down in such ancient documents as the Laws of Manu in India, in the codes of early Egypt, in the Laws of Solon in ancient Greece. These were on the whole applications of moral systems. The Romans perhaps were the first to make human rights a political concern and a responsibility of governments. But there are certain Christian views about the nature of man, which have been a powerful influence on Western notions of law and rights. If you turn to the Old Testament you will find two kinds of rights, each playing an important part in the history of Israel: what have come to be known as conventional rights and natural rights. Conventional rights are those created and protected by the customs and laws of a particular society. Natural rights are those, which are universally applicable to all men. You have an example of conventional rights in the Book of Deuteronomy, whence the father must give his first-born certain rights of inheritance, even if he is not his favourite son or the son of his favourite wife. For the most part, however, rights in the Old Testament are a protection against powerful and unscrupulous men and are natural rights. In the prophets, like Isaiah, we find denunciation of those who "take away the right of the poor of my people, that widows may be their prey, and that they may rob the fatherless". And Jeremiah complains that "the right of the needy do they not judge". Amos and Malachi remind the powerful of their time that the poor, even the strangers in their midst have rights. In the Book of Deuteronomy there is a system of moral justice to protect people against arbitrary injury. It is a body of natural rights. But there are also conventional rights like the one, by which a debtor must be let off his debt in the year of Jubilee. No modern society will allow that one.

In the New Testament our Lord claimed no rights whatever. But St. Paul referred to his civic rights when he reminded the captain of the guard that he was a Roman citizen, and therefore could not be scourged or imprisoned without trial. But while our Lord claimed no rights either for Himself or His disciples, neither He nor St. Paul absolved their followers from dutiful observance to the civic law of the Empire. They did not normally appeal to a higher law or morality to excuse disobedience. There was, however, the occasion when the Apostles, appearing before the Sanhedrin, the Jewish court, had to say: "We must obey God rather than Man". That was because the enactment of that human group was considered to be contradicting the law of religion, especially in the matter of worshipping the true God. From antiquity we have known cases where people have resisted an order of the civil ruler in the name of a higher law; they have claimed the right of disobedience. The best known example is in Sophocles' drama *Antigone*. That young woman, Antigone, claimed the unconditional right to fulfil her duty of piety and sisterly love; in her case, to give honourable burial to her brother who could receive it from no one but her. She had no enmity against the ruler of her city state, but his command, which forbade the burial, was not absolute, it was limited by the law of religion, and so she could say to the ruler Creon: "I owe a longer allegiance to the dead than to the living, and in that world I shall abide for ever. But if you will be guilty of dishonouring the laws, which the Gods have established in honour then I disobey". And she paid with her life for that conscientious disobedience. She was referring to an eternal moral order, which cannot be cancelled by the decision of a civil ruler. It is a recurring problem of good government, how to appeal to a higher law against a decision of the ruler without opening the door to a scramble for rights against decisions of civil authority. Men have only come near to a settlement of that problem when both rulers and their subjects are informed by a common religious and moral allegiance.

I said that Jesus claimed no rights. And it is often declared that Christians should have no concern for rights, but only for duties, remembering that they have no rights before God, only grateful acceptance of His mercy, which forgives our failures in duty. "If thou wilt be extreme to mark what is amiss, O Lord, who may abide it?" That is to say, if God insisted upon His right we would all be in a serious predicament. So Christianity adds a further right to all the social and civic rights of mankind—the right to receive mercy for our repented evils. But this is never quite separated from the requirement of justice. While the Christian will hesitate to claim rights for himself, except when he feels that he is typical of other men who need protection, note that Christ in the parable of the unforgiving debtor seems to say that while we may not claim *for ourselves* to have our debts repaid from another, which is our undoubted right, we must claim it for a second person against the first one. "His master called him and said to him, you wicked slave, I cancelled all that debt of yours when you entreated me. Ought you not to have taken pity on your fellow slave as I did on you?" The parable ends with the unforgiving debtor, the debtor who asked to be let off but who insisted on his rights from his own debtor, being cast into prison until he should pay the last farthing. This is to say that righteousness, which claims nothing for oneself, may for the sake of another claim everything. You may renounce your right when you yourself bear the brunt of the renunciation, but then you turn around and insist with the utmost severity that neighbour two receives what is due to him from neighbour one.

That is the Christian concern for human rights, for in public life we have to deal not with ourselves and one neighbour, but with the conflicting claims of two or more neighbours. That is the nature of the problem, which runs from domestic strains to international war. One neighbour may try to overreach another, by strength or fraud or slander; therefore society declares and enforces rights. Also the state sometimes disregards the rights of persons and smaller groups to fulfil their own proper purposes, when corporate survival is at stake. But normally it is a case of recalling the ruling power to its responsibility for the moral law by a declaration of the rights of man.

In the course of developing the idea of human rights, people in our Western society (with its roots in ancient and Christian outlooks) have come to certain fairly definite convictions about the rights of human persons. First, the right to existence (so for example a starving person was excused for stealing in order to maintain the bodily existence of himself and his family). Then, the right to liberty to pursue moral aims along the path conscience dictates; the right to choose one's religion; the right to marry according to one's choice; the right to property if it does not injure other members of the community. In brief the right to be treated as a person, not just a social convenience. Then there are the rights of man as a civil person. In the last few centuries this includes the right to some participation in government by universal suffrage; the right to share in the cultural heritage of one's community; that is the basis of education provided by society. Most important of all is the right of everyone to impartial justice in the law courts, where we expect the magistrate *truly and indifferently* to administer justice, that is to say, without any difference between one man and another. There is to be no favouritism.

My last word is this: While Christians must join with all who are working for human rights, they will never make the mistake of thinking that rights by themselves make for the improvement of human life. Many have a sense of injustice: they say they are not given their rights, they complain that they do not have a fair share of the gifts of our civilization. A very just complaint, but people are also thwarted and unhappy largely because the civilization we all want tries to make our inner emptiness exciting and interesting. Human beings project what they lack in themselves upon the system, and then say "we have not got our rights".

Let me put it in this way. A man came out of prison one day, and a friend asked him how he had got on. "Quite well", he said, "you see, I had all the four freedoms there". You may not remember the four freedoms laid down by President Roosevelt during the last war:—freedom of religion, freedom from want, freedom from fear, freedom of speech. That man in prison was quite right, he had those four freedoms. But he was not free. Why not? Because he was not able to exercise his responsibility. I am using that as a parable. The frustration that people suffer from and often attribute to their lack of rights, are largely due to their inability to use the freedom they have. They are in a prison of their own making. It is not enough to have rights; there may be other things than the lack of rights, which prevent you from fulfilling your truly human purposes. You may be free to take a walk, or to play a game, or meet a friend and intend to do so—you are deprived of no rights in these things. But when the time comes you may be in the wrong mood, you may be sulky, you may have some resentment that gets in the way of what you want to do when you have the right to do it. So the Christian should always be looking for the causes of misery, which lie within and which we are so ready to project upon those we think do not give us our rights. A healthy social order depends on there being in society a body of people who know both, which ills are due to a defective system—and there are many—but also know, which ills spring from inside men, defects, which they are always inclined to attribute to the outer world. And this should be the business of the Christian Community.

18. Justices of the Peace
To the Magistrates' Association (1970)

*"The Kingdom of Heaven is like unto a merchantman
seeking goodly pearls, who when he had found one pearl of great price,
went and sold all that he had and bought it".* (Matthew xiii.45–46)

MANKIND has been provided with three great human repair services, that of the Church, that of medicine and that of the law. It is about the last of these that I am to speak to you today, when we salute and welcome to our Cathedral worship a body of magistrates meeting to share their experiences in handling their common problems and to celebrate the fiftieth anniversary of the founding of the Magistrates' Association. And may I remind other members of this congregation that magistrates are not for the most part trained lawyers, but public-minded citizens who give their time and attention to the administration of justice in the magistrates' courts. These courts used to be called the Petty Sessions, so called because they dealt with petty criminal offences. Now additional functions are laid on them, such as acting as courts of preliminary enquiry in more serious cases. It seems to me, as a social historian, that this service of non-professional administration of the law is an admirable institution reflecting the fact that the law of the land is a responsibility, not only of specialists, but of the community of citizens. In earlier days before Robert Peel invented policemen, the men of a town did their own police duty in their spare time and thereby learnt by experience the meaning of democracy, much better than by a mass of theory. Since then society owes an incalculable debt to the magistrates who carry out the law without payment except in London and other larger cities. They richly deserve that splendid title of "Justices of the Peace".

I have referred to the law as one of the great human repair services. That was brought to my mind, back in 1917, when an acute continental philosopher declared that the soundness of a society may be estimated by the degree, to which it meets the requirements of the priest, the physician and the magistrate. That is to say, a society is the healthier—not necessarily morally more perfect—

if it facilitates rather than hinders the functioning of its spiritual, clinical and social repair services.

The Law is there because of man's imperfection, and it has its warrant from mankind's persistent endeavour to counteract and overcome its defects. Modern systems of law have an independence of religion, whereas in earlier societies law had its authority from being part of a sacred realm, which was the concern of religion. The independence of secular spheres like law, education, politics and economics, is the result of a peculiar Western history and of the Christian doctrine of creation with the world having its own spheres of knowledge and authority—a story too long to tell here. Gray's Inn in London has an endowment for an occasional sermon on "The Divine Foundations of Justice" as a reminder that all true human systems of law have their justification in the being and will of God. This does not contradict the fact that there are systems of law—and good ones, too—which have no reference to the divine foundation. But a Christian thinker on these matters has his own account of the validity of a purely secular system of law.

For such an account I have chosen as a text one of Christ's parables of the Kingdom of Heaven, the one about the pearl fisher who acquired and traded in those valued gems from the shells of sea creatures. We can let our imagination play upon his situation. By collecting, buying and selling pearls he became familiar with their qualities—became what we would call a *connoisseur*. Some pearls had good points, of weight, shape and colour, but mixed with imperfection in other respects, one was right in size but defective in shape, another splendid in sheen but under-sized. Nevertheless, by this familiarity he acquired a notion of what a perfect pearl would be like, excellent in all respects, unmixed with any fault. The parable tells that the day arrived when one specimen came his way, which at once he recognised as having this supreme quality. It is called the pearl of great price—or perhaps priceless. He went and sold all the others he had to buy that one. It was not to be bartered for others; it was not for sale, but for keeps—for enjoyment, not for use.

Among several themes we could derive from this parable, I select this one. Human justice is one of the good pearls, it has its own excellence though mixed with some imperfection, like human life itself. But there is another reality, conceived or inferred rather than observed, called in the Bible the Kingdom of Heaven, operating not by rules, laws and sanctions—but by spontaneity, freedom and love. You can call that an ideal, but for the Christian it is an ever present force brought by Christ, of which we have some glimpses, and which informs us that by comparison all our earthly justice is clumsy and inadequate.

But it is one of the goodly pearls for all that, reflecting one aspect of the pearl of great price. Men are always liable to fall into opposite errors: one is to equate human justice with the supreme good; the other to despise or rebel against it because it has not the effortless excellence human nature seems to long for. There is a great deal about this kind of excellence in the Bible. The prophet Jeremiah, in chapter xxxi, speaks of a state of life when men will no longer be subject to law. The Lord says: "I will put my law in their inward parts, and write it in their hearts". That is to say righteousness will come not by commandment, or coercion; it will be a second nature; that is a foretaste of the Kingdom of Heaven. We all know the difference between acting from our natural condition and acting from obedience to a command. A wise old priest in France once said: "The good God gave us a commandment that children should love and honour their parents, for it is not natural for them to do so; He gave no commandment that parents should love their children, for that is natural; therefore no commandment was necessary". He could have added: "that is why parents and children do not understand one another"!

We may say that justice, the commandments of society, are the will of God for man while the Kingdom of Heaven tarries. It can be put in the place of the Kingdom as if it were the ultimate truth about human relationships—then it becomes what the Bible calls an idol. The refusal to recognise any other bond between men than that of law and justice is condemned as legalism or Pharisaism, with some injustice to the Pharisees. There is nevertheless a kinship between the spontaneous harmonies of the Kingdom of Heaven and our creaking efforts to make order out of human material by means of law and justice. We must neither "divide the substance nor confound the persons" to take an analogy from a famous theological formula. If people make this mistake in one department of life they will make it in others. We find Christ saying that not one jot or tittle shall be taken from the law until all be fulfilled, but He also rebukes those who identify the letter of the law with the throne of God. And St. Paul speaks of Christ as the end of the law—meaning that in Him all that the law seeks to do is brought to completion. And yet St. Paul, who taught much about the freedom of the Christian man, nevertheless was glad to appeal to the law of the Roman Empire when he demanded to be tried by Caesar. So there is what clever people now call a "dialectical" attitude to justice in the Bible, a Yes and a No to it. A Yes, for it is the instrument of God for righteousness entrusted to fallible men—a No, when it is mistaken for the deepest level, at which God meets man—for that is the sphere of love and grace and freedom.

The place of law and systems of justice has to be affirmed against movements, which arise from time to time, where members are impressed by the impersonal character of law and offended by the need to coerce those who break it. They are the utopians, the anarchists who do not see why the Kingdom of God should not be embodied directly in this fallen world. In the days of my extreme youth a book that fired my enthusiasm was one of these utopias—William Morris's *News from Nowhere*. It was the picture of a society of the future with men and women, spontaneous, confident and brotherly, without any constraints. William Morris believed that such a society would come, and he went so far as to suggest that its care-free members might find life a little flat and would read accounts of the miseries of the nineteenth century, much as we turn to horrors as a relief from boredom. And in the eighteenth century John Wesley found that some of his followers were taking his message of Christian freedom as meaning that they need not observe moral rules and the requirements of legal justice. So Wesley preached those famous sermons entitled "The Origin, Nature and Property of Law".

Our news of today has a great deal about waves of law breaking—and there is always some of that. But now there is also a recurrence of belief in a utopian society, which has no need of law. Such a possibility ignores the contradiction in human life, which Christianity recognises and on which it bases its understanding of man. The contradiction is the plain fact that while men are often evil they are yet capable of apprehending perfection; they are made in the image of God and yet sinful. Utopianism ignores this contradiction and therefore despises the outstanding way, in which human nature has dealt with the facts of its sinfulness, egoism and imperfection, namely the idea of law and its embodiment in systems of justice. Of course the law is a burden. What a bliss it would be to live spontaneously by love and freedom. Read the accounts in the Old Testament of the rise of the kingship with Saul. The people clamoured for a sovereign law-giver and the Lord said, well, if you must have one you shall, but you will regret it. And there is the parable of the trees in the book of Judges choosing one of them to be their king. The olive tree, the fig tree, the vine all refuse to reign over the trees. The only one who accepts is the bramble, the bush, which has its fruit, but also its thorns. The thorns stand for the coercive aspect of justice, and we all at some level long to be free of it, but we cannot be free of it short of the Kingdom of Heaven. The fruit of the bramble represents the protection given to human existence from its evil and imperfection.

I am impressed with the immense *debt* society owes to magistrates; one example is the alarming increase in the amount of work coming to the courts, because society itself ceases to be self-disciplining. Consider the enormous amount of time taken in dealing with motoring offences. Not only is there the problem of adjudicating just verdicts, there is the problem of sifting evidence of the facts—and motorists seem eminently skilful in disguising the facts—to themselves as to others. A former Lord Chief Justice was asked what was his most difficult problem; he answered: "This has been my chief worry, how could two motor cars, parked on opposite sides of a broad street, in daylight, with their lights blazing and with very experienced drivers sitting at rest at their respective wheels, while being so securely parked, nevertheless collide vehemently in the centre of the road?" That mischievous and magnificent irony is a symptom of the colossal burden a disordered and self-deceiving society imposes on the magistrate, merely in the matter of ascertaining what happened.

Another example is the growing weight of judging "truly and indifferently" in a modern Western society where the magistrate is expected to go by evidence and not from his personal knowledge of the parties—a task much heavier than in a tribal society. A black native judge in South Africa said his job was becoming more difficult because people were coming in greater numbers to his court, whom he did not know. Earlier he knew them all—their situations, their habits, their truthfulness or lying power—now he had to deal impersonally with them and it became a much more onerous task. A magistrate in the great society has a much heavier job than the judge of a close-knit tribal culture.

Here is the paradox of our human situation. We must have justice, a balance of rights and duties because men do not spontaneously do the will of God. Hence the divine majesty of the law. It is a necessity of a world alienated from its true life, which is personal, intimate and free, the Kingdom of Heaven on a level, at which the burden of the law is overcome. We can put it this way: we have been cast out of Paradise, but it still exercises its pull upon us. So that life may have order, so that egoism does not destroy existence, justice is required. It is the work of the spirit of man operating in a disordered world.

This then is my attempt to welcome and salute our brethren and sisters of the Magistrates' Association on behalf of Christ Church, by a discourse on the theology of human justice. As the instrument, by which man is respected as man, human justice is the nearest expression of love in our disordered state. As such it has its own majesty, honour and glory—it is one of the best of the goodly pearls. Yet far our humility in its exercise we must always be recalled to the truth that it stands under the greater light of the Pearl of Great Price—which is the spirit of love and freedom, which proceeds from God alone.

19. Man and Nature

THAT MAN is a riddle to himself is an observation of great antiquity. It has mostly been the result of astonishment at the enigma of his inner constitution: part animal, part spirit; half determined, half free; "a thinking reed" as Pascal called him, able to order his life by thought, but also under compulsion, bending to the winds of circumstance. The unresolved puzzle of the relation between life and consciousness has provided stipends for philosophers through the ages. And now the discovery of two levels of the mind, conscious and unconscious, gives psychiatric practice the status of a healing art. In the religious and literary tradition the riddle of man was experienced as a persistent intruder into mankind's efforts to understand and direct human affairs. Here are a few scattered examples.

Leaving out for brevity the Greeks who were much preoccupied with the question: what sort of a being is this, man, who can stand back from the stream of Nature and ask the reason why, we may note how acutely the riddle of man has impressed people in the Post-Renaissance world when confidence in men's powers reached a great height. Shakespeare makes Hamlet exclaim: "What a piece of work is a man? How noble in reason... The beauty of the world! The paragon of animals! And yet, to me, what is this quintessence of dust?" and more personally "What a rogue and peasant slave am I". The eighteenth century conceived all the forces of nature to be directed in order to serve men's needs, and produced Alexander Pope's *Essay on Man* where the confidence is disturbed by doubt. He identified the human creature as:

> "Great Lord of all things, yet a prey to all;
> Sole judge of Truth, in endless error hurled;
> The glory, jest and riddle of the World".

There we have one aspect of the riddle of man, which as time goes on becomes a serious practical problem for the continuation of human life, and not only an intellectual puzzle; the problem namely of man's mastery over Nature and his dependence upon it. The mastery enhances the human condition in many respects; but refusal to observe his dependency upon it threatens the very existence of man on earth. That is the theme I wish to develop here, resisting as I must any temptation to offer a pronouncement on a necessary social policy for survival. I confine myself to showing that this form of the riddle of man has a theological interpretation.

The scriptures are not unaware of it. The eighth Psalm reveals the wonder in religious terms:

> "What is man, that thou art mindful of him? and the son of man that
> thou visitest him?
> For thou hast made him a little lower than the angels, and hast
> crowned him with glory and honour.
> Thou madest him to have dominion over the works of thy hands; thou
> hast put all things under his feet".

We may notice that the Psalmist deduces the place of man as master over things, from his place in the cosmos, as the bridge being between heaven and earth, the mediator between the creative powers of spirit and the more inert receptivity of matter and biological life. But the Psalmist-singer glories in the dominion exercised by man, without any suspicion that human dominion over nature may ever be found to have a catch in it.

The fact of man's dominating place in the world's life was given an enthusiastic salute in the twelfth century by St. Bernard of Clairvaux. In his treatise on *Man's Love towards God* he speaks of man's dignity, meaning, he writes, "free will, by which it is surely given him to rule over all other living creatures... The power of dominion demonstrates human dignity". Bernard, however, adds a warning. Beware of two kinds of ignorance: one is to think too little of oneself and ignore the dignity of dominion; the other, and the worse, is to presume on this dignity and power as if it were man's own, owing no obedience to the laws of creation. Ignorance of our powers makes us "fellows of cattle"; ignorance of our dependence, however, makes us "fellows of demons".

It is not only out of theological interest that I bring up this question of man's place in Nature—a paradoxical place indeed—but because in our region and modern age man's mastery over nature gives rise to alarming human problems. I mention only two. One is the fact that with the multiplication of man's powers, by organisation, by applied science, by technological ability, the equipment of our civilisation has acquired a momentum of its own and is in many ways destroying the sources of life. A new servitude to the mechanism replaces the older servitude to Nature, which made life so hard. See the way people talk about, for instance, the menace of increased motor traffic. In ten years' time, we hear on the journalist's gramophone record, there will be so many more millions of vehicles. Therefore, towns must be cut about, dwellings demolished, land concreted—let alone such minor calamities as deaths and injuries outnumbering the human disasters of warfare; more deafening noises and noxious vapours. All this and the like is described as something, which we have to learn to live with; exactly as if it were a change in the meteorological climate. It is talked and thought of as a part of nature, a form of belief in historical inevitability, which even Sir Isaiah Berlin omitted to notice in his famous lecture of that title. There is the threat to the life-giving power of the earth from pesticides and chemical fertilisers; water recklessly drained from its natural reservoirs, which may well reduce the fertile crescent to the condition of a desert. The rhythm of the earth's life is broken by technical ability unmatched by wisdom. Mankind may well have been commanded in the Bible to replenish the earth and subdue it. We are subduing it all right, but not replenishing it. The alarm was sounded in many works like *The Grapes of Wrath* and *The Rape of the Earth*.

The second practical reason for my raising this question is the growing depression, which arises from a sense of being stifled by the relentless encroachment of all this momentum upon the freedom of the human spirit, which freedom in fact started its growth. It is a depression, rising to revolt, not only among the young and not exclusively directed against anything in particular, but against some unidentified suffocation, which lies beyond the reach of any political programme or economic organisation to cure. It appears in fact to be a move for salvation by immersion in the stream of nature. This urge "to get away from it all" as the saying has it, is of course not new. It is a wave of the recurring tide, which took a mighty heave under the influence of Rousseau and the later Romantics. But now, the hopes of the liberal age having been defeated by incontinent mastery of Nature and the organisation it requires, men no longer believe in a social transformation such as Walt Whitman or William Morris or Karl Marx put their faith in. There is therefore an impulse to free the spirit by escape into anarchy, or complete moral permissiveness, or the sweet anodyne of narcotics. Perhaps the most inviting way out of the cramp is unfet-

tered sexuality. For it is the level of erotic love—that meeting place of personality and nature—on which men focus all their other frustrations. It is there they
find the quickest way to Nature and Mystery—from which they are cut off by
economic reason, technical domination and social climbing. Of course there is
something too self-conscious and in a way artificial in all these escapes from
the stifling artificialities of a civilization. One does not envisage any marvellous
Dionysian spontaneity in the doctrinaire members of a nudist camp. But the
urge for the simple life is the revenge of nature upon the constructions made
by the spirit of man in mastering nature. It is one of the oscillations, which
mark the career of civilized man. On the one hand men have turned with effort
and sometimes relief away from the chaos of nature, of history and the human
heart to the harmonies of reason, civil life, culture and technique. Then the
point comes when these impose their own determinisms on the soul of man;
and like the nineteenth century Romantics, people seek solace in nature and in
the past—from the constraints and aridity of a highly competent utilitarian age.

I must not be understood as contending that man's mastery over nature is
a calamity, or that it is the result of religious unbelief. It is rather that along
with the enormous benefits of the mastery in enriching human existence for us
in Western society, there goes a defeating principle, which in many ways makes
it endanger human existence. In fact, man's mastery of nature and his dominion over it is the result of an enormous religious change, which came about by
a mutation of human consciousness associated with the influence of the Bible
and Christian thought. I know this will not command assent from any of you
who believe in something called the natural development of the human mind,
or social and mental evolution. That belief seems to me a myth, by which
people now live, a secularised version of the Providence of God, a misap-
plication to history of biological evolution, plus a good conceit of us Western
peoples that we represent the main line towards the fulfilment of man's career.
I look instead for historical causes of change. Somebody or some people starts
something; history is not the same again; and if it had not been started it might
never have happened. Man's mastery over nature is one of these changes.

There is now a considerable literature about the origin of the impulse to
change man's environment and the aptitudes necessary for it. It seems to have
come about when a breach was made in the human consciousness between
man and his world. Where the ancient faiths of the Near East held that man is
part of society, society is part of Nature and Nature is Divine—there was only
participation and not confrontation between man and nature—Hebrew mono-
theism placed man in direct relation to the transcendent God, who is the

source of being, the lord of history and the creator of nature. The world is no longer the mediator between man and God; man meets Nature with a basis and a warrant from beyond Nature. The heavens may declare the glory of God but they are not He. "He sitteth above even the Cherubim, be the earth never so unquiet". The dissociation of man and nature has made possible man's enterprise in understanding and manipulating the natural world. It has made possible the great wave of experimental and theoretical science in the West. True, the Greek philosophers had made some dissociation of mind and nature; there had bean empirical technical inventions in the Far East, but there was no great impulse to change the world until the Bible view of the universe as a creation, with history moving towards a goal, was carried into the Christian Church and European culture. This monotheistic view meant that the world was a universe; the principle of unity was not, however, in the world but behind it. Also, because only the Lord was holy, nothing in creation was too sacred to touch. The world could be studied and handled with laws of its own, without referring every thing and movement to the First Divine cause.

The Bible does not show very much interest in Nature for itself. The Old and New Scriptures make plentiful use of the natural world as illustrations and parables and sometimes as models, like the lilies of the field. For the most part the sub-human world is valued only for its use to mankind. The creatures are there to serve man.

Besides this effect of a particular theological world-view, there came another influence for encouraging man's dominion over Nature. By emphasising the unique and powerful forces of man's inner life, his spirit, made in God's image, and in a delegated way sharing in God's creative and re-creative power, great trends were at work to develop those inner powers of man. The ascetics in hermitage and monastery sought to master nature inside men, sometimes stretching it to grotesque lengths. But without this development, Western man would have remained very much a creature at the mercy of the natural forces. This damming up of man's natural vitality produced a steam, which in later ages was directed outward on to the physical world. The modern University and the Laboratory are the cultural descendant of the monastery. The vanquishing of nature within man led to the conquest of nature outside man. Nature does not do science, the starfish does not write theses for a D.Phil. on marine biology. Only man performs this extraordinary activity.

This interpretation of the impulse to master nature as related to a religious world-view may seem ridiculous in view of the alleged conflicts between Christianity and science since the 17th century. But there have often been conflicts or serious misunderstandings between parents and offspring. However, it is not my own interpretation. I have support for it in, for example, the work of the physicist Carl Friedrich von Weizsäcker (*The Relevance of Science*), in the philosopher Karl Jaspers (*The Origin and Goal of History*), in the Dutch Calvinist van Leeuwen (*Christianity in World History*), in the Russian Nikolai Berdyaev (*The Meaning of History*). Berdyaev called man's liberation from the thrall of nature "The death of the great Pan". He writes: "As long as man had found himself in communion with nature and had based his life upon mythology, he could not raise himself above nature by means of the natural sciences or technique... Christianity had freed him from subjection to nature and had set him up spiritually in the centre of the created world". This is not contradicted by the effect of the Copernican revolution, which showed that physically he is not the centre. Berdyaev discerns the danger of de-animating nature by treating it as a slave, and exclaims: "We need now a higher degree of spirituality, which would enable man to commune once more with the mysteries of cosmic life without having to submit to the determinism of its forces".

There were indeed many Christian theologians who sought to elucidate the spiritual significance of nature, like Gregory of Nyssa and Scotus Erigena. And you will not overlook the devotion St. Francis of Assisi showed to the natural world. But one has to say that the popularity of St. Francis has been largely based on a mistake. People feel sympathy for one who deserted houses and cities for the open road, the sun and the air. Especially they are attracted to his love of his fellow creatures, and then they quite wrongly regard him as a nature lover, or an emancipated soul who fled away from the ecclesiastical side of Christianity, or put him down with those undeveloped misfits who say "the more I see of men the more I like dogs". Of course Francis loved the animals and all natural things; he preached to the birds; converted the wolf of Gubbio and sang the lauds of the creatures. But he was not a nature lover in the usual sense; nor did he find God in nature. He loved and respected natural things as creatures and servants of God. It is quite clear that Francis' love of creatures was a supernatural love that returned to creatures by way of God, after the spiritual revolution of giving up the hold they had on him. His love for the birds, the animals, even "sister death of the body", was a kind of courtesy, which contains reverence and respect, as when he addressed the fire, which was to cauterise his eyes: "Brother fire, you are good and strong and beautiful, I pray you be courteous with me". He appears to have had no inkling of mankind's possible abuse of nature. But his follower Bonaventura had, for in his *Hymn of Creation* he makes created things, the earth, the water, the air, cry out against man:

"This is he who abused us... Why must we bear upon us this monster? Why do we not deprive him of our benefits?"

And if you want someone more modern to underline the enigmatic character of man's dominion over nature, here is our contemporary Albert Schweitzer, theologian, musician, physician and missionary, telling us: "By the power we obtain over the forces of nature we do indeed free ourselves from nature, and make her serviceable to us, but at the same time we thereby also cut ourselves loose from her, and slip into conditions of life, the unnatural character, of which brings with it dangers of many sorts".

20. The Things that Belong to Peace

"If thou hadst known the things that belong unto peace".
(Luke xix.42)

IT IS NOT Christianity, which says that peace is better than strife. Nearly everybody thinks that, even those who are on the point of starting a quarrel or a war. What Christianity does is to give the aim of peace, which nearly all people hold, a religious foundation. There is, you could say, a Christian philosophy of peace, and it is not a bit like that of the world. In fact, the characteristic Christian word—its gospel—lies not in its contrast to the wicked world but to the good world. The world has many high and human aims without the Christian revelation. And in this matter of peace the Christian has a different diagnosis and different resources for carrying out the good aims of men.

The world has produced many elaborate devices for preserving or restoring peace such as international law, alliances, pacts and the United Nations, for in this imperfect world peace and harmony require organisation and force to combat unscrupulousness. The message, which peoples are offered, is usually one of three dreary platitudes. They are told that conflict inheres in separateness, as if nearness and likeness make for harmony, whereas a little distance frequently avoids cantankerous strains. Or they are told that peace and concord are in their better interests than war or strife; if only men were brothers—so runs the gramophone record—if only they recognised how dependent they are on one another then we should be well on the way to a harmonious world. A third illusion is that there is not enough peace and unity because men do not desire them enough. We really do not need politicians or administrators or ecclesiastics to tell us these things. We know them all right, and it is a poor use of Christian resources to repeat such trite hypothetical statements. Merely to know that harmony is blessed and conflict a curse does not make for peace, as anyone on the brink of a domestic squabble or a professional row can tell you.

The sayings about peace in the New Testament do not assume, as the well meaning world assumes, that the desire for peace is the cause of it, or that if conflict arises it is because people have not desired it enough. The gospel is offered, in fact because of a single premiss, that to want the good does not bring it about. There have to be some resources in the soul or in a community, which back up and sustain men's good aims. That is what St. Paul explains about the need of his own divided self before he was made into a unified man by the power of the spirit of life in Christ Jesus. That is what our Lord himself declared what was wrong with his brethren by race of the city of Jerusalem. They no doubt wanted peace and, like all of us, that means the kind of peace we want—on our own terms. But they did not know the conditions of peace and therefore could not discern, which of the social and political forces were the most threatening to their stability. It is a striking cry, this lament over Jerusalem; Jesus did not finish the sentence. But it contained the main theme I am seeking to expound, namely that those who want peace must attend to the forces, which lead to peace. It was indeed a hard saying to a small people who had for centuries been under pressure or oppression from great world powers. But the theme has a wider application and has been expounded by teachers in perhaps less strident circumstances. The author of *The Imitation of Christ* has ventured to say this precisely: "All men want peace, but not all want the conditions that belong unto peace".

In most of the places where this blessed state of peace is mentioned in the New Testament it is spoken of as a gift, not as something brought about by human striving alone. We read of "the gospel of peace", as if peace is one of the results of believing the good news that God redeems His people. It is one of the fruits of the Spirit, along with love and joy. The Apostles are offered His peace by Jesus on the eve of that unspeakable conflict, which was His passion. "My peace I give unto you". Every time harmony between men, which is all that most people mean by peace, is hinted at in the gospel, this harmony takes second place, as a sort of by-product of the peace between man and God. And there is a further New Testament message, namely, only when a man is at peace with God is he at peace inside himself. What is more, so long as he is not at peace inside himself he is sure to get at loggerheads with others. Conflicts between men derive from disharmonies within men. That is not always obvious. At first sight it looks as if it is only plain, single, uncomplicated egoism, which gives rise to oppositions and conflicts. Two or more people want the same thing. Some want other people's land or wealth or employment, or husbands or wives, or social advantage. Or people want different things when they could be pulling together—which is the

bane of many a family holiday. There are certainly plain conflicts of self-will between people. But if that were all, the human race might have managed pretty
well to curb its worst results by governments, laws and other forms of discipline.
What makes peace a really difficult and tricky achievement is the existence of
another kind of conflict; it arises not because men want to quarrel or make war
or to have what another has, but because conflict is something they are driven to
by conflicts within themselves. That is what St. James means in his epistle when
he writes of wars and rumours of wars springing up from the desires that "war in
your members", the conflicting or frustrated aims within the same people. This
applies to families, to classes and to nations as well as to individuals. St. Augustine tells us in his *Confessions* how as a boy he got into conflict with his neighbour for stealing pears from the neighbour's orchard. But he did not want the
pears; he threw them away. In later life he knew why he had done this, namely to
get a sense of power over the man next door, to overcome what people nowadays
would call an inferiority feeling.

In brief, this diagnosis points to the interior disorders, which lead to external disharmony between people who do not deliberately want to be at variance
with others. It is another case of "the divided will", which St. Paul and St. Augustine describe in terms of the single person. On this point too Abelard writes:
"the fact is that this kind of will, existing with much internal regret, is not, if
I may say so, will, but a passive submission of the mind. It is so because the
man wills one thing on account of another. He puts up with *this* because he
really desires *that*". The submission of the mind to conflict is made not because
it wants *this*, namely conflict, but because it wants *that*. *That* may include, for
instance, the overcoming of frustrations in the personal sphere, political divisions in the social sphere, and economic disbalance in the economic sphere. In
the small circles of life we know this by experience. We wake up in the morning
on the wrong side of the bed, or we get irritated, and then we take it out on
someone not in the least involved. Many a marriage or family discord begins
when one member suffers from being out of joint with his or her work or with
their social mates outside. And many a war has started not because a people or
government saw what a lot they would get out of it, but because it saw or
thought that it would get it out of a lot of other difficulties.

The specific Christian doctrine of peace, then, rests upon the premiss that
in order to be a good neighbour, I must be at peace in myself, and in order to
be at peace in myself I must find my fulfilment in God. Otherwise we expect
our neighbour somehow to minister to our lack, to come to our rescue, to behave in this or that way, to give us a certain consideration or whatever it may

be. And when the neighbour is not ready to be used as a convenience in this way—and why should he—then we are resentful, and he resents our resentment, and so conflict grows.

It would not be too difficult to apply this same diagnosis to conflicts in the wider sphere of world affairs. Nations, classes or groups of peoples suffer from internal troubles or disharmonies, and then it seems as if the troubles always come from outside; the rest of the world or society is behaving badly; and to counteract that peace is destroyed and rivalry aggravated. But these are matters beyond the scope of a sermon, and I would not have you think that because I do not include them I am concealing my conviction that there are many valid causes for breaking up certain kinds of peace because [they] are unjust.

Theologians in the past have seen some of the tragic nature of the conflicts, which destroy peace—tragic in the sense that men are driven into conflict, which they do not will, by hidden forces they do not understand. That is in refreshing contrast to the monotonous patter today about the need to strengthen the will to peace. Look at St. Augustine's chapter 12 of *The City of God* (Book XIX) There he expounds what he points out in one sentence, as follows: "They that perturb the peace they live in, do it not for hate of it, but to show their power in alteration of it". And Thomas Aquinas, commenting on this book of Augustine, says that behind the break-up of concord, namely strife, there lies a defective peace, in which it is the conflicting purposes of the same men that lead to conflicts between men: "Concord, properly speaking, is between one man and another, so far as the will of various hearts agree together as consenting to the same thing. Now the heart of one man may happen to tend to diverse things... but the union of such appetites is essential to peace, because man's heart is not at peace so long as he has not what he wants, or if having what he wants, there still remains something for him to want, and which he cannot have at the same time". Aquinas does not fully work out the connection between the conflict of purposes in the same men and the destruction of concord, which is strife between men. But the Anglican matins Collect picks up this connection and, using a phrase of St. Paul, speaks of God as the author of peace and the lover of concord. The harmony between, which is concord, is pleasing to God; but it requires as its root condition a harmony within men. That harmony man himself cannot bring about however much he believes in the advantage of its results. Man's life only reaches the true kind of unity, which does not go exploiting around when it finds its significance and fulfilment in God. Only then can a man look at his neighbour without wanting something of him, that is, without being, perhaps unwittingly, a cause of strife.

21. Nations as Neighbours

"The rulers of the people dwelt at Jerusalem,
the rest of the people also cast lots,
to bring one of ten to dwell in Jerusalem,
the holy city, and nine parts to dwell in other cities".
(Nehemiah xi.1)

PUBLIC-SPIRITED men have lately been adding to church observance some commemorations expressing hopes and needs of human society. So you will find an annual Sunday allocated to thought and prayer for the United Nations. This body was formed after the Second World War and it replaced the older League of Nations as an international device to preserve and extend peace in the world, by law if possible, but if not, then by some accredited force. The idea grew out of the alliance of the victorious powers and has now membership of many other nations as well.

Reflecting upon this organisation for supporting the aim of world peace, I thought how similar is its structure, though on a much vaster scale, to the attempt in Israel, after the return from exile in Babylon, to maintain unity among disordered and unruly Israelites who were setting up village and town communities from scratch again.

They chose one out of ten in each of the scattered regions and brought him to Jerusalem in expectation, no doubt, that this representative minority would act as an influence for unity throughout the whole collection of Jewish peoples who were learning to become a nation again. Apparently their original racial stock was not sufficient to make a harmonious civil whole of returning exiles tempted to grasp property and power. It is likely that the songs and sighs for unity in the later Old Testament come out of this situation, such as Psalm cxxxiii: "Behold how good and pleasant it is for brethren to dwell together in unity".

And notice that the returned population did not rely only upon the longing for peace; they knew that men's desires are often tricky and deceitful. So they devised an organisation where representatives in the holy city would learn unity by a common effort to carry out the Lord's purpose for His people, and to build together the material and civil fabric of the community. Let us, all these centuries later, see what we can learn from our faith about nations and the conditions of peace and unity among peoples.

There are several popular delusions about peace and unity. One is that men become more co-operative as they grow out of a state of nature red in tooth and claw. That is quite disproved by natural and human history. Then, there is another view, that the unity of mankind is the extension of unities in smaller groups like the family or city. No! Men in group loyalties can be more hostile to other groups than their individual members to one another. "Never", said the wise philosopher, Henri Bergson, "shall we pass from the closed society to the open society, from the city to humanity, by any mere broadening out. The two things are not of the same essence". We could add something from Ecclesiastes: "The mercy of a man is upon his neighbour; but the mercy of the Lord is upon all flesh".

If we are to consider the meaning of the nation in terms of the Bible and theology, we may say that it belongs not to the order of nature nor to the order of grace, but to the order of history. Nationality is a state of life, to which some peoples are called in certain circumstances of their earthly careers—then they get what we call "a history". A nation is a body of people united by geographical togetherness, by a share in the same history, and by the rubbing together of ideas and purposes. It has thereby reached some kind of common view about the order of value and importance in its interests, activities and loyalties. It has often been formed by including people of different blood, language and territory through an invitation or a coercion by one group of men to carry out some enterprise in common. Renan defined it: "In the past, an inheritance of glories and regrets; in the future one and the same programme to carry out. The existence of a nation is a daily plebiscite".

The word "nation" occurs frequently in our English Bible, when it renders the Greek ἔθνος [ethnos] and the Hebrew term for a race or people; and there is a great difference between a people as understood in the ancient world, and the nation as we understand it, which emerged in the fifteenth century when the two translocal powers of empire and Church began to lose their unifying force. At this point let us turn to St. Paul's famous passage recorded in Acts xvii: "Seeing that God is the Lord of heaven and earth, He hath made of one all nations of men for to dwell on the face of the earth, having determined their appointed seasons, and the bounds of their habitations, that they should seek God, if haply they might feel after Him and find Him". In his play, *St. Joan*, Bernard Shaw pointedly illustrates how strange was the new idea of nationality less than four hundred years ago.

Nevertheless, nations in the modern sense have some of the same ingredients as "the peoples" of the old world—both denote well defined human "groupings" each with common roots in nature and history. So we can apply some things, which are said of "the people", to the nations of our own time. St. Paul begins with the common humanity, to which the separate peoples belong. He emphasises the universal aspect of mankind, which must never be absent from the Christian's thought about history. "And hath made out of one, all nations of men". Then he goes on to say that the differentiation of this one mankind is also in the purpose of God, though it is not a supreme purpose, which should crush out every other. Nations have a real meaning for human destiny, but nationality is not the final or absolute truth about human life, to which everything else is relative. "He hath determined their appointed seasons", that is, He fixed the epochs of their history. They have their career in time, with a rise and development and disappearance. They are not eternal, though they last longer than the life of a man or a generation.

Secondly, "He hath determined the bounds of their habitations", that is, He fixed the limits of their territory. They have their place, being a people who live upon a certain part of the earth's surface. On it they depend for their physical sustenance. Even if they send away some of its products for others. And this carries a responsibility for tending and husbanding the patch of earth, on which a people live. Modern nations are forgetting this. But, the moral of a nation being set within the bounds of its habitation, is that it is limited in space and has a responsibility to the place, on which it stands. The earth, like God who gave it, cannot be exploited indefinitely without penalty.

And now, there is a third thing St. Paul says about the nations "that in them men should seek God if haply they might feel after Him and find Him". He speaks of a sense of mission, which a nation must discover if it is to fulfil the purpose of God for it. That is why a goal of mere self-preservation, or peace, or prosperity is never a motive vital enough to ensure that a people will remain a true nation through its appointed season. There has to be a conviction of making a contribution to the spiritual and cultural stock of mankind. That is the meaning of being chosen in the Old Testament, chosen, or elect, for a purpose. The Lord regards only the nation's appointed task and no preferences. He sends prophets when the people do not walk in His ways or do not listen to His laws, and pours out over them the fury of His anger. He even uses hostile peoples as a scourge in His hand, as when He speaks of "my servant Assyria". The choice of a people is the choosing for a mission. Isaiah makes the Lord say: "Is it too light a thing that thou shouldest be my servant to raise up the tribes of Jacob and to restore the preserved of Israel". Yes, there is to be something more: "I will also give thee for a light to the Gentiles, that thou mayest be my salvation unto the end of the earth". There were then two lessons to be drawn from this idea of a people chosen. One, that the covenant is not a favoured-nation clause in the treaty God makes with man. The Jews often behaved as if it were. And today great nations, if they are also strong, as well as young nations aspiring to become states, act and think as if God's will is finally and absolutely embodied in their survival and power in the world. There is no higher law, by which they judge themselves than the necessities of their own control over others and this is usually disguised in the moral mantle of offering the truly human life for all men. The Jews had to be undeceived about this by their tribulation and in their exile away from the paraphernalia of their accustomed religion; learning that the Lord was still their God even when they could not sing His song in a strange land and when all familiar links were snapped. They had to learn the universalism of mankind behind the call to be a special nation.

The second lesson about being called to be one people is the way God wills that local excellences be mutually beneficial. The truths learned and the aptitudes acquired in one national community move outward, they spread from a centre. A people, which has learnt from its teachers and its own history, can then be a vehicle for the transfer of its excellences to others, or take its part in the variegated riches of diversity. This is overlooked or denied by a false universalism, which holds that a part of mankind, a nation or a local community, cannot get nearer to its true pattern under God, unless there is a world-wide solution of the whole human problem. Some Christians are apt to think that because modern national growths divided up the unity of Christendom, therefore if only nations were superseded by some more world-wide groupings, such a new world would have the same appeal to Christians as in the pre-national period. They forget this difference: then there was a universal religion in Europe, a semi-Christian Empire—whereas politics, industry and culture were mostly local. Today we have an universal economic culture, which is tending to iron out all local character and habits and in which the supreme values of religious faith are private and not social in their effects. And where so many international forces are parasitic upon the peoples they affect, there may well be only social harm from extending their power. Of course, the abuses of nationalism are more dangerous than those of individualism because in them the egoism of sinful man is more easily disguised as a community purpose. But no Christian will believe that the existence of well-defined national groups is by itself more likely to cause conflict, than the existence of separate individuals causes quarrels. It depends on what they say and do to one another. All through human life distinctness and separateness are as often occasions of collaboration as they are of strife.

Of course, where there is no common or moral standard, by which the peoples could rebuild policies, there is always the danger of the nation becoming a false god, an idol. But to replace nations by greater power groups—or by horizontal divisions of interest will merely re-group the interests of sinful man. Over and over again internationally-minded people ask: "Should nations survive?" If we as Christians ask that question in terms of God's will for men in this historic situation, I would answer in this way: the fact of nationality, which reached its greatest strength in the nineteenth century, is still, in spite of its perversions, a counter-balance in the divine providence to greater end more deceptive idolatries. Because men's social consciousness is limited in its range, it is of concern to Christians that the groupings, in which human loyalties are collected, should not be too far removed from the control of their members. And they should not be so vast that their power cannot be checked by other similar groupings, and should not be so extensive that they no longer represent the local communities within them. Nationality has not yet exhausted its contribution to the resources of mankind, and all alternatives on the map seem to involve more unmanageable clusters of power.

To return in conclusion to the word of the Lord, we find several allusions to the nations in the Book of Revelation, that revolutionary pamphlet, which closes the Bible. It speaks with two voices. One declares that there is something wrought out in the history of the several peoples that become part of their destiny *sub specie aeternitatis*. "The Glory of God does lighten the eternal city; and the nations shall walk amidst the light thereof: and the kings of the earth do bring their glory into it". The other word is of judgment upon the nations, carried out by Him who is called Faithful and True and is also called the Word of God, who hath on His garment and on His thigh the name written King of Kings and Lord of Lords. "Out of His mouth proceedeth a sharp sword, that with it He should smite the nations: and He shall rule them with a rod of iron". What do these two voices say? Simply this, the first speaks of the reality of nations in the purposes of God—He does not mean mankind to be merged into some kind of standardised cosmopolitanism. The second voice says what a terrible thing it is when this good of nations becomes an idol in the place of God. National purposes are right, but they are not supreme, subordinating all other human goals to themselves. There is behind the separate nations the unity of mankind and therefore men are called, besides their nationality, to a deeper and wider community, the Church of the living God representing the universal oneness of mankind.

v. COMMEMORATIONS

22. St. Frideswide

"Thou bearest not the root, but the root thee".
(Romans xi.18)

THIS IS ONE of the frequent analogies made in the Scriptures between human achievement and the process of growth in vegetation in men or society, for human affairs contain certain sudden changes, revolutions, conversions, destructions and conflicts, as well as growth. But this imagery of growth from a stem to a root, does remind us that what we are and what we do now is not merely the result of our decisions and ability in the present, but the consequence of two forces meeting together. One of these forces comprises the purposes of habits of mankind at any one period; the other the religious, intellectual and civic history, which each period inherits from the past, what we call our culture. And when I use the word culture I refer not only to the literature, arts and refinements of life, but the whole growth of the present; its work-life, its politics, education and set of values, in which we are rooted, without knowing most of the time that it is an inheritance. This complex of our heritage is usefully called our culture. The very word is derived from husbandry, but is now also used in chemistry and biology, to indicate that what we are talking about is a growth that requires tending, like a farm or a garden, and if it is not tended it runs to weeds or jungle or desert.

We are today keeping the feast of St. Frideswide, the obscure woman saint of the eighth century, who in spite of vagueness in our knowledge of her person and deeds, has collected round her name and place the dedication of three massive institutions of present-day Oxford: the City, the University, and this Cathedral and College. All three of these institutions have for centuries held her as their common patron saint. The idea of a patron saint derives from the days when Christian people believed firmly in the Communion of Saints, in the sense of the whole family of the Church, on earth, in purgatory and in heaven, being united in a fellowship of prayer. The patron was the saint, chosen by tra-

dition or otherwise, as the special intercessor, and advocate in the near presence of God, of a particular place, person or organisation. St. Frideswide intended nothing of the three institutions of town, university and cathedral
church of Christ in Oxford. They have chosen her, not she them. It was not
until 1434, seven centuries after her settling and then presiding over a community of nuns, and probably monks as well, that Archbishop Chichele of Canterbury ordered the probable date of her death, October 19th, to be observed
for her commemoration as patroness of the University.

A natural curiosity makes us wish to know more about this woman, her
character and doings. Where so much is legendary, a great deal is left to the
imagination, and none the worse for that. Such imagination obviously inspired
our Burne Jones east window in the Latin Chapel, too crowded to be of great
artistic merit. No wonder the visitor from France, when told the window represented events in the life of St. Frideswide, exclaimed: "Mon Dieu, she must
have had a very busy life".

Historically speaking, there is very scanty evidence. What there is has been
splendidly sifted in two publications edited by our lamented late Dr. Cross, and
published here as St. Frideswide Papers, one by Professor Jacob and the other
by Sir Frank Stenton, and then marvellously distilled by Dr. Myres.

We can, I think, infer something about St. Frideswide from what she
brought about by just settling her community here. Only someone of considerable influence becomes clustered round with legends. It appears she was a lady
of rank, one of the minor royalties of those days, and with something of
a haughty disposition, which impelled her father to endow a site and nunnery
of her own, instead of her joining another sisterhood in a humbler station. But
it was not all worldliness that moved her, for she refused marriage to a royal
suitor whom she treated somewhat brusquely. Probably she objected to being
pestered, and we can only guess that in the experience of ruling a conventual
society, and of course submitting to its discipline, she learnt the kind of forceful
humility, which often grows in a personality of some power. Dr. Claude Jenkins
used to say: "It is wonderful what the grace of God will do!"

Frideswide's mortal remains were not for centuries allowed a resting place.
After at least two translations, they now lie, in all probability, under the marked
place in the north east of this cathedral church, along with the remains of Mrs.
Peter Martyr. The bones of the eighth century Catholic prioress and of the six-
teenth-century convert to the Protestant reformation now repose together in
ecumenical quietus.

If our knowledge of St. Frideswide herself is rather dim, we know a good deal about her period, in some ways a very fruitful period in the history of Church and society, disturbed though it was. The spread of Christianity south-ward had been stopped by the power of Islam; Africa and the Mediterranean world were largely cut off. So Christianity went north, and by a long and pain-ful missionary effort a new Anglo-Saxon culture was created. Literary education spread through monastic houses. It was the age of the Venerable Bede, writing his great *Ecclesiastical History of the English People* on the south bank of the Tyne. It was the age of Irish and Anglo-Saxon missionaries, like St. Boniface who carried this literary religious culture to the Germanic peoples. The English Church was for a time the greatest force in European scholarship. Besides, a school of decorative sculpture arose and declined. It was in that period that the body of Old English poetry began to take shape. "St. Frideswide herself", wrote Sir Frank Stenton, "may be little more than a name, but the age, to which tradition assigned her, was the period, in which the English Church exercised the deepest influence on the learning and religion of Western Europe". All this was going on almost a century before King Alfred fought the Danes and burnt the cakes and translated Boethius from the Latin. How much of this vitality was fostered in priories like that of St. Frideswide, I am not enough of a historian to say. There was of course no university in our sense for some time, but the seeds were there. Students in monastic houses went back to their own districts and carried their learning with them. There must have been some kind of small township here in St. Frideswide's day. Owing to its place on the river, Oxford was a kind of border between kingdoms. The convenient passage over the Thames for the ox, pictured on our city crest looking like a beast stepping on to a switchback at St. Giles' Fair, made for a growing civic life. Perhaps that is why this place was chosen for St. Frideswide's priory.

I have given a very imperfect account of the geographical and religious, civil and intellectual root, from which sprang the three institutions observing St. Frideswide's festival at this time, namely the City, the University and our own Christ Church. Here in Christ Church history has produced a quite unique graft of two stems. Nowhere else in the world has a college grown on to half of a priory church, which has now become a college chapel and the cathe-dral of a modern diocese. We today stand on the spot where Frideswide's search for a site began it all. Perhaps the blessed Frideswide, peering through space and time, and observing what has been going on in this first week of a new term, might well exclaim: "Good heavens, did I start all that? It never entered my head!" And she may well request the heavenly choir to sing the words of Cowper's hymn *God moves in a mysterious way*:

> "Deep in unfathomable mines
> Of never-failing skill
> He treasures up His bright designs
> And works His sovereign will".

23. All Souls College

I LOVE the shape of things. So when I am asked to preach a commemoration sermon to this venerable society at the season of its dedication, as an outsider I come wondering: what is the shape of this place? And by shape I do not mean physical shape, with the Hawksmoor Towers, the Codrington Library or this Chapel. I mean your institution with its historically grown uniqueness. So unique that in the words of a famous guide book "All Souls remains an anomaly"—but not much more of an anomaly than Christ Church. And when I have finished explaining to an eager inquirer from abroad first what are colleges, then what is Christ Church, I am thankful I do not have to go on to All Souls.

My attempt to respond to your invitation has meant for me a little voyage of discovery, and you will allow a visitor a certain thrill at what must be the familiar background of your lives. I have long ago ceased to believe that things, institutions and modes of thought come about through some natural development of the human mind. No, things happen because someone—or many—started them. Nothing is the same afterwards, and they might never have occurred but for that one historical origin. If therefore your society is an anomaly, may it never be anything else! With its oddity crushed out by the standardizing operation of the abstract intellect.

I ponder with the eyes of a tourist upon the shape and history of your institution: a college and at the same time a chantry. A college retaining some of the character of what all colleges were originally, according to Hastings Rashdall: "primarily a body of students and not a body of teachers". Today in particular I am bound to recall two features of the shape of All Souls; its regular commemoration of the Founders, Benefactors, bygone Wardens and Fellows, and of all who have served it in various capacities; secondly, the Dedication of your society, expressed in your official name: Collegium Omnium Fidelium Defunctorum. Firstly then your invitation has made me reflect on the question: what is a commemoration? It is not an act of memory in the ordinary sense of digging out from the dormitories of the soul impressions, which once were wakeful, but then were tucked away until revived by some stimulus or other. We never knew most of those who envisaged, built, paid for, endowed, and laboured to make, All Souls what it is. To commemorate is a much more deliberate act than to remember. It is an *anamnesis*, a calling to mind all that has been done and—though I am doubtful whether there is such a thing as a group memory—what has *been done* is part of our present, and we salute it. But theologically, a commemoration is an act of piety; it is taking a backward-looking stance; a regular act, not only signifying a society's gratitude to its domestic past, but a symbolic redressing of that bias in modern society, which regards being for-ward-looking as the only truly human attitude. We need both attitudes. I believe De Tocqueville was right in saying: "As the past has ceased to throw light on the future, the mind of man wanders in obscurity". Therefore, there are moments when it is laid upon us to stop attending to what we stand for, and to turn round and recall what we stand on. That is an act of piety, and for all the modern debasement of the word it denotes one of the two essential movements of the Christian life, the other being the human spirit's activity seeking to make the future. "Spirituality looks to the end, towards which we move—it is the aspiring side of religion and morals—it desires to know and to do the works of God—it strives. Piety on the other hand is man's reverent attachment to the sources of his being and the steadying of life by that attachment. This con-sciousness that the human spirit is derived and responsible, that all its func-tions are heritages and trusts involves a sentiment of gratitude and duty, which we call piety" (George Santayana). Every age has its strong and its weak side. Ours is weak in its conscious sense of indebtedness—but under its feverish activism it seeks nourishment in the historians' drama of the past.

The *pietas*, which our commemoration brings to a point, was of course a disposition valued in the pre-Christian Graeco-Roman world, which we may perhaps have derided in Aeneas if and when we read our Virgil. But in that world *pietas* was not so much a feeling as a vocation and a duty. Men were called upon to treasure and know the ground, from which they sprang, and the resources, which upheld them, what they stood on in order to bring about what they stood for.

It would be tantalising to explore what a Commemoration like this implies about our feeling for the passage of time. But we must not be led astray. I note, however, that Mr. J.B. Priestley is one of the latest explorers to put the riddle of time again before our minds—a "time-haunted man" he calls himself. In that he is one with the human race, which in its earlier rituals sought to overcome the fateful succession, in which nothing transient can be recalled. I wonder how Mr. Priestley would react to Wren's inscription on your sundial: "They (the moments) pass away and are counted against us". Perhaps, commemorative *pietas* is one of the ways, in which time-haunted men make friends with the fearsome ticking away of every present moment, for as we commemorate we take the past into the bosom of our living present. For support in my musing on these things I quote Thomas Carlyle—breaking my own rule that the young should read him between the ages of 18 and 20 and not after.

This rambling old word-monger was very cross about many things in his own day and wanted them changed, but he had an intense reverence and gratitude for what had been given. Here are words from *Past and Present*, which make a bridge between your Commemoration and your Dedication: "The Past is a dim indubitable fact; the Future too is one, only dimmer; nay properly it is the same fact in a new dress and development. For the present holds in it both the whole past and the whole future—as the life-tree *Igdrasil* (in the Norse legends) wide-waving, many-toned, has its roots deep down in the death King-doms, among the oldest dead dust of men, and with its boughs reaches always beyond the stars; and in all times and places is one and the same life-tree".

And now, your dedication to the memory of All Souls, especially of those who died in the wars, makes your institution a living monument to one of the most influential forces in Western history. I refer to the cult and ritual of All the Faithful Departed. This has a history and a beginning: it represents an out-standing mutation not only in the Church's story, but also in that of European society. Christians had always prayed for their departed, their relatives, their friends and their connexions; men had remembered their abbeys, houses and civil bodies before God. But not before the 10th century was a day set apart for *omnes omnimodo fideles* and added to the Feast of All Saints. It is impossible to exaggerate the change of temper this represented. Compare it with, for exam-ple, the mood, in which one theologian of the fifth century, in the heat of doc-trinal controversy, referred to the death of Cyril of Alexandria:

> "At last with a final struggle the villain has passed away. Observing that his malice increased daily and injured the body of the Church, the governor of our souls has lopped him off like a canker... His departure delights the survivors, but possibly disheartens the dead; there is fear

that under the provocation of his company they may send him back to us again".

What a contrast when Odilo of Cluny, at the turn of the 10th-11th centuries, conceived the idea of begging on the hill of purgatory for all souls ever born or to be born. The liturgy of All Souls, only to be completed two centuries later, established in the hearts of men the *solidarity* of all believers from the beginning to the end of time. This spiritual solidarity, over-arching all barriers of historical groupings, had in it an element of universality. This is why, as it seems to me, it made such an appeal to generations painfully aware of local feuds, and who held in mind the old lost Empire with its relative universality, as a remembrance and a desire. Earthly life is local, parochial, particular and fragmentary. So, largely, had been the monastic houses. Cluny, where the commemoration of All Souls was cradled, achieved an organizational expression of universality by starting to become itself a trans-local order. Further, the Frankish Emperor, as distinct from local prince and lord of manor, wandering round with a traveling court and army, like an Eastern shepherd or Abraham with his tent, seemed to stand for something corresponding to this same hope of a universal allegiance wider than the local bonds.

Then, of course, the significance of All Souls Day cannot be separated from the *Last Judgment*. Because of the mutation in Christian consciousness expressed by the commemoration of all departed, the Last Judgment became no longer just a matter of personal and ecclesiastical belief, but now also a public acknowledgement of great sociological consequence. While much modern political thought holds that men are born equal and has often made a pretty mess of trying to squeeze human realities to fit the theory, Christendom inaugurated the idea that they die equal. All Souls is possibly the source of all recent warrants for a universal community of equals—for all the perversions of that hope. The *Dies Irae* can be regarded as the hymn of the equality of all souls before God at the great accountancy of the dead. It appears that you as a college in earlier days appropriately timed your financial audit for All Souls-tide.

I have read of a late ritual in Austria, in which the corpse of the Emperor was ordered to be carried to the door of an abbey. The chamberlain who leads the cortege knocks at the door. A friar opens the window and asks: "Who knocks?"—"The Emperor". "I know of no man of that name". The chamberlain knocks again. "Who's there?". "The Emperor Francis Joseph". "We do not know him". Third knock and the same question. The chamberlain now answers

"Brother Francis". Then the door opens to receive a comrade in the army of death, on equal terms with all the other souls. In death and before judgment, the smallest is the equal of the greatest.

And now one more contribution to the spiritual shock of European humanity, which comes out of this whole setting. Besides solidarity and equality, the significance of particular individuals is given a new context when, as in the ritual of All Souls and later in Dante, the Christian consciousness draws a line, as it were, from each particular individual existence to his place in the universe, which lies beyond the visible organisations on earth. Within a decade of your foundation charter in 1438, Nicholas of Cusa was elaborating in his *Visio Dei* an analogy of the actual presence of God to all creatures alike. The image is that of an *eikon*, which seems to be looking at you and him and them, and all at once, wherever they are, and so, in a parable of uniqueness, plays havoc with our spatial or arithmetical thinking. Let one monk fix his eye on the *eikon*:

> "And while he observeth how that gaze never quitteth any, he sees that it taketh such diligent care of each one who findeth himself observed as though it cared only for him, and for no other... He will also see that it taketh the same most diligent care of the least of creatures as of the greatest, and of the whole universe".

There you have this same insight that informed the commemoration of All Souls, and gave it a sustaining power. Thereby the Last Judgment was not all terror, but also a recognition of the dignity of man who is not a weed or a rag to be cast out when functionally finished, but a being God thinks highly enough of to fix His eyes upon him and call him to judgment.

I have offered you a halting expression of fascination at what your dedication in part means. It matters not only to your own foundation but to the cultural religious history of mankind. Take this offering, please, as a fraternal salutation to your august College on its commemoration anniversary.

24. Opus Dei at St. Paul's (1947)

W HEN the public hears about St. Paul's Cathedral it is usually because a royal or state occasion is being celebrated, or a largely attended special service is to be held, or because the cathedral's architecture or structure is under consideration. In this last matter my predecessor in the office of Cathedral Treasurer, Canon S.A. Alexander, who died last February, had spent the best part of a lifetime as custodian of the fabric and its treasures. He kept attention on St. Paul's by informing the world about every problem, change and achievement connected with the cathedral. And at the present time both church people and the general public are interested in proposed changes at the east end of the interior.

The Dean and Chapter will continue to make known what is being done in and around St. Paul's as construction proceeds. But as St. Paul's gets into the news mainly as a place for special services or as a public monument, I want here to recall the more regular rendering of divine worship, which goes on there without much public attention. It is this, which makes the foundation, or centre, or skeleton (whichever metaphor you prefer) of all that happens in the cathedral. The day-to-day recitation of the divine office and celebration of the Holy Eucharist are the life of the cathedral. But, like the parabolic mustard tree, which exists to bring forth its own fruit and nevertheless lives also to shelter the birds, St. Paul's is privileged to serve the Church and nation in other ways.

One of those other ways has been followed by St. Paul's just being there. It is well known how during the war its survival was a source of confidence and hope, and how it was a symbol of persistence amidst destruction. Englishmen, and Londoners in particular, felt that St. Paul's was a kind of fixed point, by which other things could be measured. That sense had been caught and expressed before. Chesterton wrote a fantasy called A *Nightmare*. It described an iconoclastic and "scientific" architect exploding some sticks of dynamite in the crypt of St. Paul's:

> "The next moment this dome that filled the sky shook as in an earthquake, and tilted sideways. Nothing could express the enormous unreason of that familiar scene silently gone wrong. I awoke to hear the hoarse voice of the yawning man, speaking for the first and last time in my ear. 'Do you see', he whispered, 'the sky is crooked?'"

There is another testimony to the same impression, made soon after the cathedral was completed. An uncanny prophecy seems to have prognosticated its present situation. It occurs in some poorish verse by a young nobleman (Thomas, second Baron Lyttleton, 1744–1779) in a letter dated 2199 to a friend in Boston on the state of England and the once flourishing City of London [*The State of England in the Year 2199*]:

> "These were my thoughts whilst thro' a falling heap
> Of shapeless ruins far and wide diffus'd,
> Paul's great Cathedral, from her solid base,
> High, tow'ring to the sky, by heav'n's command,
> Amidst the universal waste preserv'd
> Struck my astonished view!"

To turn from this widest significance that St. Paul's has by just being there, to its general public functions, it fulfils three purposes, which are not always easy to coordinate or to make mutually reinforcing. In the first place St. Paul's is the Cathedral Church of the diocese of London, the *cathedra* of the bishop. This is hardly realized by many who visit and use or read about St. Paul's Cathedral. Secondly, it is the largest London church with close connexions with the City of London. Lastly, the cathedral is a national and imperial shrine as well as a kind of spiritual centre of gravity for the whole English-speaking world. So it holds the interest, the respect and the affection of countless men and women of many lands.

St. Paul's has no parish, but it has its permanent constituency, namely the whole staff of the institution. This comprises the Dean and four residentiary canons, four minor canons, Choir School staff, gentlemen and boys of the choir, two organists, a Receiver and a Surveyor, four vergers, several guides, the Clerk of Works and his deputies, stonemasons, carpenters, plumbers, painters, electricians, scaffolders, watchmen and others. The work of all these people has to be co-ordinated and if the arrangements for a large special service are envisaged, together with the problems of post-war reconstruction in the building and its surroundings, some idea can be reached of the problem of administering the cathedral. And one of the humbler reasons for the performance of *Opus Dei* at St. Paul's is that it provides the clerical staff with the duty of worshipping together as a corporate body. Any priest worth his salt knows the value of obligations to attend to prayer and praise in preventing him becoming a pottering busybody. This is a particularly necessary exercise for those who have to deal with the multifarious problems of cathedral life. In the case of St. Paul's, which, in addition to all the rest, is thronged with visitors, these problems are of a peculiar distracting character. And the more decorous, dignified and august the impression made on visiting worshippers, the more attention is required behind the scenes.

I use the term *Opus Dei* in the wider sense of the regular round of worship, including the Eucharist and the two daily offices, though St. Benedict, who seems to have invented the phrase, did so to describe only the hours of prayer, which he did so much to make an integral part of the Church's life. It is these monastic offices, compressed into the two services of Morning and Evening Prayer, that are now regarded by most people as the "proper" Church of England services.

Now, St. Paul's can perform all the functions required of it without being enfeebled or distracted by many of them, only because at the heart of all its activities there goes on the day-to-day offering of divine worship. Here, very nearly, you can see Anglican worship carried out according to the intention of the Book of Common Prayer, and that is almost the best thing St. Paul's can do. By the attraction it exercises upon visitors to London and many a half-churchman who turns up now and then, it can teach by what people see and hear going on there.

Apart from a few aberrations, the services of the Holy Communion, Morning and Evening Prayer are rendered intact. A cathedral can afford to order its worship by standards of excellence, without concern for the circumstances, which a parish priest has to some extent to observe. Two ways, in which we endeavour to carry out this purpose, are illustrated by the two following statements.

The first is a letter received this year by the Dean from an unnamed Country Parson. It ran:

"I recently had an opportunity to attend evensong on a week-day afternoon at St. Paul's, a cathedral, to which I have great devotion as the scene of my own ordination. Probably the officiating clergy and still more the choir feel that the cost of maintaining these splendid services is wasted before so small a congregation. I know if I was a choirman I would think so. But I can assure you that to a country parson like myself the experience of a nobly performed service in London's cathedral is a thrill, which probably nothing on earth can give, and which inspires one to make new efforts to improve the quality of our village worship. On the other hand, an unworthy performance in St. Paul's would be a terrible shock, I can imagine. The other day in St. Paul's I sincerely thanked God that such worship was carried on".

The second statement was made to me by one of our deputy minor canons. One day in the period of the blitz Mattins was being said in the Chapel of St. Dunstan, when the Dean, all the canons and minor canons (except those who were on active service) were present—and the congregation numbered just one. The solitary lay worshipper was a well-known judge who had dropped in to St. Paul's on his way to the Old Bailey. A few days later the judge met this deputy minor canon and said to him:

"Padre, I had a wonderful experience the other morning. I don't often get an opportunity of going to St. Paul's, but when I do, I like to say my prayers there. I was amazed to find in these dangerous days the entire clerical staff of St. Paul's going through the whole service—I was going to say, for one person. But I realize that the service would have gone on just the same whether there had been a thousand present or no one at all; for it was only by accident that there was even one in the congregation. It was an eye-opener to me. The service would be offered every day even though bombs were falling, and whether the congregation numbered ten thousand or none. It was a new idea to me, that the service was rendered not for a congregation—but for Almighty God".

A cathedral, and perhaps especially St. Paul's, has in a way to be something of all things to all men without losing its character as a cathedral of the historic, Catholic and Apostolic Church. It can be a little accommodating in its special and national services without detriment to its Church character if the regular cycle of liturgical worship is kept up with faithfulness and with such excellence as we can give it. In this respect a cathedral with its special resources should be the place in the Church where liturgy, music and (God forgive us) preaching can be seen and heard at their best. It might well be a school of religion where instruction and conference and spiritual direction take place. And there are many ways, in which the vast throng of people who come in and out of St. Paul's as sightseers can be helped by what they casually see and hear to sense the reality behind the Church's service and architecture. Underlying all this is that exercise in "the sanctification of time", which consists in the daily offering of the Eucharist, with the recitation of Morning and Evening Prayer, in the mother church of each diocese as in every parish of the Church militant.

These acts of worship are exercises in love and obedience, for in them we follow a sequence of Bible lessons, psaltery and liturgical action, which runs in a cycle based upon the annual revolution of time and its subdivisions, interspersed by variations due to the feasts and fasts commemorating the Christian drama of redemption. *Opus Dei* is not topical: it uses a somewhat archaic language and it commemorates eternal facts in the historic context of Christ and the Bible. It bids us listen and pray and offer sacrifice and communicate in a context and with an idiom, which belongs to periods in the past; so that it can the better be a vehicle of the unchanging significance of the redemptive acts of God. It is pathetic how all attempts to devise an idiom of worship for today, almost in a night appear to be using the idiom of the day before yesterday. In *Opus Dei* we use the language of the Church; we pray prayers, recite psalms, hear scriptures, make Eucharist, in words and actions, which do not naturally reflect *our* motives just then. Therein we subordinate our temporary and fleeting religious moods and needs to the more recurring themes of Christian spirituality. That is the priestly aspect of worship. Topical expressions of piety are valid. Prayers, intentions, supplications and the spoken word about the world and the soul at this and that time are one proper exercise of the living Church, they express its prophetic mission. But if that were all we should fail to reach the deeper, the more abiding and the more searching level of man's existence— for at this level every man and every age have much the same religious predicaments and resources. The Christian can only interpret his situation now as under God, when he hears what is said to him at this moment from God whom he has learned to listen to and to be one with by familiarity with God's perennial and recurring word to all men and all times.

To provide a standard and norm for this kind of ministry is something, which St. Paul's Cathedral pre-eminently can do, and to which all the other functions it performs can be referred back for their significance.

VI. OBITUARIES

25. William Temple, Archbishop of Canterbury

"The Lord is my light, and my salvation;
whom then shall I fear?"
(Psalm xxvii.1)

IT OUGHT to be a long time before we get over the sense, not only of immense loss, but of calamity, that has been forced on us by the death of William Temple, our Archbishop. Yet, in order to make this blow prod us to greater faith, fidelity and power in Christ—as indeed we must—it is not too early to search reverently and gladly for the hidden springs of William Temple's amazing influence. Let me take you a step or two in that search, which I have tried to begin.

Consider for a moment what a unique position he filled in the confluence of Church and Society, which has a peculiar embodiment in England. The death of this Archbishop will cause a feeling of unreplenishable void in the hearts of thousands outside the Church of which he was, for the last two and a half years, the chief pastor, and for much longer than that the supreme genius. Many who have talked to me since the announcement of his passing, and to whom an archbishop does not mean very much, express sentiments not only of heavy loss but of calamity. There goes one of the very few, they seem to say, in our critical and bewildered society, on whom in the last resort we could rely for a judgment and a stand based upon conviction, clear reason and moral integrity. And this sentiment is uttered by people to whom some of the Archbishop's views and policies have seemed misguided. The hold, which the personality of William Temple has taken upon the affection, the respect and the trust of the English people is a phenomenon, the significance of which it is too early to assess. It was evident already in the merciless demand made upon him from the moment he succeeded to the primatial throne of Canterbury, demands from religious and cultural organisations and secular causes—demands seldom refused—which came to him on top of his responsibility to be the spiritual voice of the nation on every critical and outstanding public occasion. These were not demands for official patronage, but demands of a commonly unsatisfied need for clarification, for guidance, and for principle before policy. When the resources for meeting such a need in the soul of a people are embodied in a man deemed fit to occupy the first spiritual office of the land, we reach one of the high points when the idea of an established Church seems to be justified and given a reality, which is doubtfully evident in the intervening periods.

One asks, therefore, what point in the rich pattern of Christian truth such a man finds most significant; what is the central fact, for him, round which the others cohere and to the glory of which they contribute? I think that for William Temple it is the truth of God as Light. As I try to detect the dominant theme, which formed his mind and religion and which moulded his character, I am sent at once to the Psalmist's hymn: "The Lord is my light and my salvation: whom then shall I fear?" The metaphor of light as expressing the most intimate, compelling, central aspect of God's being and His action in relation to creatures, was dear to the mind of William Temple. Here he stands in the great classical Christian and Catholic tradition, with the *philosophia perennis* and not with the modernists for whom life, or love is more ultimate.

There is a sermon of his, delivered at Cambridge in 1927, in which be expounded how theology has its own warrant and way of grasping reality—a way independent of science—more like the approach of art; more like a concrete, visual, direct penetration into meaning than a comprehension by abstract conceptions and general laws, with which science has and ought to work. The addresses at his mission to Oxford, published under the title *Faith and Life*, were each preceded by the prayer: "O Thou who art the light of the minds that know Thee, the life of souls that love Thee". And when he is illustrating the meaning of the Cross and Redemption, and making the contrast between the price of remaking man through the agony of the passion and the naturalness of creation, the words that occur to him for the latter idea are "Let there be light".

Temple had caught the emphasis of the scholastics on the beatific vision in terms of Light, of sight, which causes love. For love, in all creatures but God, is a striving—not an absolute satisfaction—until it is fulfilled in the *visio Dei*. This, you may know, was expressed by Dante in Canto xxvii of the *Paradiso*: "And thou shouldest know that all have their delight in measure as their sight sinketh more and more into the truth wherein every intellect is stilled. Hence may be seen how the being blessed is founded on the act that seeth, not that, which loveth, which after followeth".

Love kindled by light. Temple induced warmth and enthusiasm by the light he shed, never by setting out to produce heat. He was what they call a dynamic personality, that is to say, he provoked movement in the thought and soul of others. But he did this precisely by offering light, and this made him kindle energy that comes from receiving light. It was not the damp, unhealthy heat that comes when men offer warmth. Temple never spoke of "spiritual dynamic" or imagined ha was helping anyone by saying how very much we all need it, which is the mark of contemporary spiritual ineffectiveness.

This gift of kindling energy by shedding light is what made William Temple a great teacher. And I think that his great influence as a prelate was due to the fact that behind all his other gifts there was his power to teach men things. He was never merely the administrator, or the public leader, or the episcopal chief. Men went to him for these things because he always had something to give them. And, like a good teacher, he never talked down to anyone.

Outstanding among his teaching pronouncements were the addresses he gave, as President, to the Manchester Diocesan Conference, mostly published in his *Essays in Christian Politics*. These essays include such diverse subjects as *Coué and St. Paul*, dealing with the relation of the will, the imagination and the work of Christ. Another essay on *The Resources of Literature* has a section on limericks. In another, he discusses the tension between the Catholic and the Reformation elements in the Anglican Tradition. And he could speak most personally even in such general statements. For instance: "When we try to do things, we fret over our incapacity and are anxious. But when we fix our minds on the eternal goodness, we gain both strength and peace; and the peace, which we find becomes a protection against all that would detract or debase". Temple interpreted the office of a Bishop as that of being the first teacher of the Faith in his diocese. He had put himself to school with Charles Gore to learn more of the Bible, and to a member of a religious order to know more about prayer. No wonder that the clergy in his diocese went annually to school with him enthusiastically, because they wanted to, not out of a heroically pumped-up loyalty or political discretion.

As a philosopher he used, during the formative years of his thought, an idiom, which we do not find satisfactory now. I refer to his statement of truth in terms of values. But when we find him interpreting, say the Real Presence or the Incarnation, in terms of Values, we must consider it with the same attitude as he brought to his estimate of the language of *substance* and *accidents*, in connection with the Holy Sacrament. What the thinkers meant was true, says Temple; what they were trying to safeguard was essential, though that is not the way *we* can think about the inner truth of things.

It was painful to disagree with him on matters, which brought out deep personal convictions, because he was always ready to see that one may have had hold on something he might have missed. I disagreed with him on the relation of Faith and Order in connection with what I believe to be spurious moves for Reunion. I think he detached Faith and Order too much from each other. But I know that Archbishop Temple believed that the Apostolic Ministry was essential to the reality of the Christian Church. The point of difference arose when it was a question whether a particular scheme of Church union did or did not impart the Apostolic Ministry.

He seldom spoke of his own experiences and preferred to display his mind on the things his friends and hearers were concerned about. But one personal record he had made may fittingly be added:

> "Do not think me egoistical if I give you one experience of my own. I had to make a choice, which I found very difficult. I was much interested in the work I was doing, believing it to be of some value. I was asked to take up another post, which certainly was more conspicuous in the eyes of the world. I tried to avoid it. I asked all the friends of whom I could think, and they all said I had better stay where I was. I had to make a decision in time to write a letter by a certain post, and, having weighed up the question as carefully as I could—and we must always do that—and having come to no conclusion at all, I began at eight o'clock in the evening to say my prayers, and for three hours, without a pause, I tried to concentrate all my desires on knowing clearly what was God's will for me. I do not know how those three hours went; they did not seem very long, but when eleven o'clock struck I knew perfectly well what I had got to do, and that was to accept; and I have never had a shadow of doubt since that it was right".

Some of us who knew William Temple only fairly closely, would be bold enough to make our own, in our estimate of him, the prayer said by the third priest in T.S. Eliot's *Murder in the Cathedral* about St. Thomas à Becket: "O my Lord, the glory of whose new state is hidden from us, pray for us in your charity; now in the sight of God, conjoined with all the saints and martyrs gone before you. Remember us. Let our thanks ascend to God, who has given us another saint in Canterbury".

Of no one can we say with greater certainty than of William Temple that we are uttering the deepest longing of his soul when we make the petition "Let Light perpetual shine upon him".

26. Michael Beresford Foster, Student of Christ Church

CHRIST CHURCH mourns today over the loss of one of its senior members, Mr. Michael Foster. Whatever may be said of him later and better, on this first Sunday after his death a tribute is due to his memory. He was known and loved and respected not only by his pupils, by his academic colleagues and the domestic staff of the College, but also by many members of the University outside these walls, as well as by men and women of the general public. What is more, this esteem very often grew out of an immense gratitude, which many, both young and older, feel they owe to Michael Foster, for his understanding, his sympathy, and for the trouble he took in helping them spiritually or intellectually, or with just deep personal concern for their problems.

Those of you to whom he may be only a name, must therefore forgive us for using this sermon period in order to voice briefly what we feel we have lost so suddenly. Indeed, it may not be so difficult for a general congregation to allow us this domestic privilege, because, as I hope I may help you to see, there is a sermon to be found in Michael Foster's life and teaching and struggles.

All who knew him well, and mostly those who found their Christian faith through him or had it strengthened, were aware that his own faith—which he came to lateish in life after a period of agnosticism—was maintained only through a recurring struggle against practical doubt, and this is what made him such a wonderful kindler of faith in others. You know, there are two types of Christians who have conveyed to their fellow men the resources of Christian faith, and the Lord uses both types in His own way. One type seems favouritely blessed by Almighty God; their faith is a steady, unruffled, strong assurance, which carries them across the dark patches leaving no deep spiritual scars. Such were in modern times men like John Wesley and Archbishop William Temple. The other type is used by God, almost unmercifully it seems to us;

they cannot relinquish the faith, to which they have committed themselves, but for them it is not one of "the consolations of religion", it is a heroic struggle to hold on with the will to obedience and discipleship, when often their thoughts and feelings seem to say they are God-forsaken. John Henry Newman was, I think, one of these, and so was Bishop Charles Gore. These men acquire a seminal and robust kind of certainty, all the stronger for the pressure of practical doubt, especially doubt of their own acceptance by their Lord and Master. Michael Foster was one of these. I was privileged to have his confidence from time to time in moments of deep depression, which afflicted him. The roots of that recurring melancholia were never clear to me or perhaps to him; and it would be impertinent and irreverent to probe too deeply. I can only say that I have a terrible sense of failure, in that I was only able to restore his confidence for limited periods. I think it is a testimony to the depth and reality of his faith that it gave him over and over again a desolating sense that he was betraying it. Of the three theological virtues he had faith and charity in abundance; but somehow there frequently occurred a hitch just where faith spills over into the virtue of hope.

Perhaps, if he had met wider Christian influences after his conversion, he would have been able to see his repeated dejection as part of "the dark night of the soul", which when first met seems as if it means that God has taken Himself away from us into a far country, but when understood becomes a means of assurance that God holds us in our very being in spite of leaving our thoughts and feelings bereft of a sense of His presence.

I would say that Michael Foster came by a hair's breadth only short of complete sanctity; he had all the marks of holiness but just missed the joy of the saints. Yet, note how the Lord used him. In the two days since he died I, and at least one of my colleagues on the Chapter, have received messages of condolence from people—odd people about town, and university dons here and elsewhere—who say that they owe their faith and their soul to him. Isn't it as if, in a way, the Lord sometimes laid upon him the doubt and desolation he was removing from others, like the suffering servant? He was taking their burdens upon himself, and in his great humility frequently thinking that he himself was the castaway. I was about to describe him as a heroic soul, but he would not have liked that, for he tells us in his book *Mystery and Philosophy* that heroism is not a Christian virtue. The heroic man prays: "Lead me into temptation so that I may test out the power of the good in me" he quotes from Bonhoeffer. But the Christian prays: "Lead me not into temptation", the fiery trials, which I may not be able to stand. If then we may not call him a heroic soul, we can certainly say that his was a sacrificial life; he gave to others what he could not all the time ensure for himself, namely the assurance that he was accepted of God.

This man endured the Cross in himself; he could have avoided that by relinquishing his commitment to Christ. He was one of those on whom tribulation comes "because of the Word", as our Lord said in explaining the Parable of the Sower. But, unlike the men whom Jesus there described, Michael never shirked the tribulations by going back when he had once put his hand to the plough. That is how the Lord uses some of his most faithful servants. As for most of the rest of us, for whom our faith is a calm certitude or a shallower and painless contentment, well! we may be thankful that God has used us mercifully, and we have our own kind of ministry. But we are not of very much use to Him; we haven't suffered enough in our faith. We get the blessing, which Jacob received without having had to wrestle with the Angel of the Lord.

We must then thank God for this sacrificial life. I would have conventionally said that it has been cut off too soon. But a letter I received corrects me, and I now see with greater insight. It is from a lady in this University, and she puts the matter in a different light. She writes: "Rather it seems to me that it was a great grace that allowed someone as heavily burdened with unresolved sorrows as Michael Foster was, to continue so courageously and faithfully for so long".

He must have been one of the best loved university teachers in the whole country. We loved him here, though he tried us sometimes by turning a direct practical problem into a tense moral dilemma. He was at the disposal of pupils and outsiders who came to him for guidance and got it. He was also at the mercy of unhappy people with a grudge against life or against others, and he agonised over whether perhaps they had not been victims of injustice. Here again is the sacrificial life in action.

I have touched on these solemn and religious aspects of our dear colleague's life, and I know that he would wish me to say these things now, which if they had been said in his lifetime, it would have been telling secrets.

There are other things. Of his work as a teacher of philosophy I am not the man to speak, nor is this the place. But two aspects of his work strike me as adding to the picture of his mind and personality. A good many years ago Michael Foster wrote some articles in a philosophical journal on the origin of the scientific impulse in Western civilisation, and connected it with the world outlook brought about by the influence of the Bible and Christian Theology. This apparently paradoxical thesis has been quoted over and over again by others who have shown its importance by building upon it. But Michael never seemed to think they were of much importance or value, and did not take up the matter again.

The second thing I have in mind is the way Foster would handle a purely secular subject like Political Theory, respecting its autonomy as a secular discipline, and at the same time making clear that a Christian thinker must see its meaning as a worldly matter in the light of God's providence. He never brought in religion as a pinch of piety to sweeten up worldly concerns. He sought to place secular things like government or science—those, which belong to this Age, this *saeculum* between Creation and the Last Day—to place them in a framework fashioned by God. Michael never encouraged people to go about being pietistic when they were meant to be scientific or political. But he strove to suggest that secular things were an essential element in God's world.

Today is the Feast of St. Luke the Evangelist, who gave us the Third Gospel and the Acts of the Apostles. He tells us in the preface to his Gospel what he was after. It was to give to his readers—personified as one, Theophilus, lover of God—an assurance that the faith they were living by was grounded in evidence, which could be tested. He did it by finding out and collecting all that was known about the Christ. Luke himself had not been an apostle or an eye-witness, but he went for his information to those who could testify. Thus he gave us what is in some ways the fullest, best written and most moving account of the strange happenings, which started our faith.

Michael Foster too wanted students and scholars to find the same kind of assurance in testing what they believed, and this was to be done, not by running to the Bible or theology or the Church between times, but by pursuing the things they were studying as if the pursuit were a vocation. His own life was a vocation, and a costly one to himself.

To God's gracious mercy we commit him;
and may light eternal shine upon him.

27. Thomas Stearns Eliot, Poet (1965)

W<small>E ARE</small> here as a congregation to express our fellowship before God with Thomas Stearns Eliot in the place where he worshipped and served as Churchwarden for many years. It is therefore a domestic occasion for those of us who mourn the loss of a brother in Christ, humbly and gladly grateful to have shared the Faith with the greatest poet of his day and the most invigorating interpreter of this age to itself. To make our homage and supplication match at all the scale of his contribution would be impossible. Let us instead reflect upon the difference, which his poetry, his thought and his presence ought to have made to our understanding of the Christian religion. Far beyond the circle of those who knew him personally, his was a presence, which was felt by countless people as a kind of "blessing"; without him we feel bereft of some sustaining power. Rarely have art and thinking and integrity been so welded together in a single mind. Of his eminence as a man of letters, as a philosopher, and as a prober into the mysterious explosive significance of everyday things, no one can yet make an estimate. Nor is this the occasion, and I am not the man to try.

What we can perhaps attempt is a diffident appraisal of what in our Christian fellowship Eliot should mean to us, who now commend his valiant and sensitive soul into the hands of a faithful Creator and merciful Redeemer. His most influential poem, *The Waste Land*, was written before be became a member of the Church. There he wrestled with the problem of his inner and outer world, the outer world of the later nineteen-twenties. The poet Auden, addressing Eliot on his sixtieth birthday, says of *The Waste Land*:

> "It was you
> Who, not speechless with shock by finding
> the right language for thirst and fear,
> did most to prevent a panic".

And here is how E.M. Forster in his curious way testified to the effect of the early poet. He spoke of Eliot as one "who could turn aside from the gigantic horror (of the post-first war world) to complain of ladies and drawing rooms and preserve a tiny drop of our self-respect; he carried on the human heritage... Still when I read him it is for the witty resentment followed by the pinch of glory".

And only the other day a poet in Liverpool, Mr. Adrian Henri, opened a poem *In Memoriam T.S. Eliot*, with this:

> "I'd been out the night before and hadn't seen the papers or the telly,
> And the next day in a café someone told me you were dead,
> And it was as if a favourite distant uncle had died".

Putting these three voices together, we may say it comes to this: The man who prevented a panic of the human spirit, by voicing the despair and perplexity of his time and giving it a meaning, "suffering us not to mock ourselves with falsehood", by taking that despair into himself, finding it echoed in his own private agonies, was naming it all with his superb gift of words, setting it as part of the universal human predicament, and then following every resentment of it with a pinch of glory. And, what is more, his astringent poetry, disallowing all illusions, becomes beneficent like a favourite distant uncle. Indeed, his younger friends naturally dropped into the habit of calling him "Uncle Tom".

We do not know the origins of genius; nor can we explain what a poem means, for the poem gives the meaning to those who work for it. Has not Eliot himself said: "Art does not represent a philosophy, but replaces it". What logical thought cannot say, poetry can, but in such a way that the reader has to play his part.

For all his alleged aloofness, Eliot paid his readers the compliment of enlisting their co-operation. He said that most religious poetry was second rate, and so easily feigned an emotion, which is not there to give body to the words and to move the will. I, who am no poet at all, remember talking with him about this necessary come-back from the reader. (I think we'd both been reading Dorothy Sayers' book on the Trinity, *The Mind and the Maker*). Eliot and I agreed that the hearers' essential co-operation in the fulfilment of a work of art was something of an analogy to the work of the Holy Spirit in the Christian life, by which God opens the mind to listen and appropriate what is revealed in the Son, the Word disclosing the secret of the unknown GOD.

The need to elicit this response may have something to do with what are called the difficulties of Eliot's poetry, its cryptogrammatic method, the sudden switch of images, the opposition of the sublime and the trivial: "Spinoza and the smell of cooking" was his own expression; but we could make them up ourselves, like for instance "Dante's *Divine Comedy* and badly rolled up tubes of toothpaste in bathrooms". I mention this demand, which he knew he made upon readers, stinging them awake by his cryptic way of speaking—I mention it because he came to see how its validity could be interpreted in the light of Trinitarian doctrine.

In the same way one of our conversations brought out, at least for me, something of the meaning of "inspiration". Where I then lived, in Amen Court, we were listening to a broadcast about same of Eliot's poetry and drama. The young speaker at one point said, this is what those lines mean. Afterwards Eliot said very quietly: "I did not know I meant that, but perhaps there was that meaning in it". That was not in the least said ironically, for he knew that something takes hold of our conscious intention when "we wrestle with words and meanings" and comes through to the hearer via the speaker who is then a kind of vehicle. As we talked of these things we both thought that in the vocabulary of Christianity this is what inspiration means.

If I were asked what was Eliot's fundamental striving, I would say it was to identify the contradiction of human existence, and by mastering it in words, to that extent begin to overcome it. In his poems, his dramas and his literary essays, he reverts over and over again to the dissociations or even the clashes between valid parts of our life: between for instance the idea and the reality, thought and sensibility, emotion and outward profession. Between these things there is a rift or an opposition. In *The Hollow Men* he speaks of it as the shadow:

> "Between the idea   Between the conception
> And the reality   And the creation
> Between the motion   Between the emotion
> And the act   And the response
> Falls the Shadow   Falls the Shadow".

It seems to me that Eliot's sense of desolation at the mutual betrayal of emotion and response, which latterly he saw as one result of the Fall of Man, enabled him to perform the greatest service to the Christian world of our time. He disinfected it from sentimentality and cliché. No fake emotion must be tolerated, and it was perhaps because of his disgust at bogus sensibility that his poetry, even in *The Rock* and in the *Four Quartets* gave the impression to many like Yeats and E.M. Forster (at first) and others, that it was deficient in feeling, especially religious feeling. Yes, he certainly was suspicious of what is commonly called religious experience. But note how he evaluated authentic emotion. In an early essay, on Philip Massinger, he wrote:

> "What may be considered corrupt or decadent in the morals of Massinger is not an alteration or diminution of morals; it is simply the disappearance of all personal and real emotions, which this morality supported... As soon as the emotions disappear the morality, which ordered them, appears hideous. Puritanism itself became repulsive only when it appeared as the survival of a restraint after the feelings, which it restrained, had gone".

So much for moral pose without genuine feeling. On the other hand, emotion to be real must go out to its proper object. In Eliot's essay on Hamlet he wrote: "The only way of expressing emotion in the form of art is by finding [and here is Eliot in one of his more donnish moments] 'an objective correlative'; in other words, a set of objects, a situation, a chain of events, which shall be the formula of that *particular* emotion". Along this line of thought Eliot came to the conviction that religious emotion without GOD as the object of faith, was really a pathological condition. In this sense only would he have endorsed the demand in some quarters today for a "religionless Christianity". But those who call out that slogan do not, I'm afraid, mean what he would mean.

There was, I think, an exhibition of bogus emotion in some angry reactions to Eliot's play *The Cocktail Party*. I am not referring to the revulsion against the dramatist who gave Celia a death by crucifixion—a revulsion in people who say nevertheless that a poet should face life as it is—and of course things like crucifixions do take place now. It may have been a dramatic mistake, but it was not a falsifying of reality. I am thinking rather of the spurious indignation aroused because the estranged husband and wife, after their infidelities, are not allowed by the play to find a glorious and ecstatic reconciliation, but just a good and tolerable partnership. Good heavens! What sort of paradise do people think they are in, the loss of whose glories appears to them so despicable. They despise the ordinary good life, which they make little effort to reach, because it has not the ineffable rapture of the saints! I have always felt that there was a good deal of humbug in the charge that to allow two levels of Christian attainment, the moral and the sanctified, is to turn the first into a kind of low gear religion.

In that play Celia chooses the hard way of sanctity and renunciation. She is asked—are you sure you don't want the more modest and ordinary good life where people

> "Maintain themselves by the common routine,
> Learn to avoid excessive expectation,
> Become tolerant of themselves and others,
> Giving and taking, in the usual actions,
> What there is to give and take…
> It is a good life. Though you will not know how good
> Till you come to the end. But you will want nothing else,
> And the other life will be only like a book
> You have read once, and lost. In a world of lunacy,
> Violence, stupidity, greed… it is a good life".

Now with such little insight into his mind as my clumsy words may have conveyed, let us turn again to the man himself. When young people who find out that I knew him ask me about him I say: you must find out some things for yourselves; for example why Eliot considered the blasphemies of Marlowe and the satanism of Baudelaire to be more Christian than the somnambulist religious pronouncements of the devout. When they ask me to explain Eliot's enormous influence, I can only answer: find out for yourselves that he was a revolutionary force because he was a traditionalist. Progressives never start a new direction: they only go faster along the same old groove.

There was of course a human and intimate side to this powerful figure. He could be playful, as when in the company of friends where I was present in a restaurant, Eliot ordered ice cream with hot chocolate sauce. One of our group, Mr. Geoffrey Davies, exclaimed: "Eliot, I cannot imagine how a poet can enjoy that revolting mixture!" "Oh that", said Eliot, "is just because you are not a poet. I have no difficulty in imagining it".

At another time I talked in Germany to students after Eliot had been there to lecture. They were crushed and raw and terribly mixed up, not only from the horrors they had been through but also from an unavowed guilt feeling. They told me that nowhere but in the poetry of Eliot did they find any cathartic, healing word, "so courageous to confront the dark elements of experience" to quote Lord David Cecil's description. Tom Eliot teased those German students when they pestered him to say whether Harry, in *The Family Reunion*, killed his wife or not. "Come on, tell us". "Do you really want to know?" "Yes, we do". The answer: "I haven't the faintest idea".

Then there was a pleasing devilment in him occasionally. It might have been after some desolating talk by an ecclesiastic who identified what he liked to believe with the operation of the Holy Ghost, that Eliot was provoked to exclaim: "The spirit killeth: the letter giveth life". Actually it was after reading Shaw and Wells (Footnote to essay: *Baudelaire in Our Time*).

In his writing he handled the deepest religious themes without the usual conventional religious language. Such were the stripping of the false self and the recovery of the true self; death and resurrection; the state of desolation on the way to enlightenment. And withal keeping himself out of the way. Hence his great humility, his sincerity, which Dr. Helen Gardner, one of his most perceptive critics, said was what he had taught her most—the meaning of sincerity.

He has left us nothing in the nature of an apologia, nor an account of his conversion. I know, however, that in his religion and probably in his conversion he found himself under compulsion, chosen rather than choosing. The Revd. Frank Hillier, to whom Eliot used to go for confession and spiritual direction after the death of Father Philip Bacon, writes to me: "Eliot had, along with that full grown stature of mind, a truly child-like heart—the result of his sense of dependence on GOD. And along with it he had the sense of responsibility to GOD for the use of his talents. To his refinedness of character is due the fact that like his poetry he himself was not easily understood—but unbelievers always recognized his faith".

As a publisher, Eliot had to read a lot of disturbing literature, but it did not have the effect of shaking any of the deeper foundations of his faith. Another friend, Mr. Philip Mairet, says of him: "A man of philosophic training, his religious position was bound to have extensive intellectual outworks. And then, his generosity caused him to befriend so many men in the universe of letters, including some big ones, who were remote in opinion from him, and whom he made efforts to understand and do justice to". Mr. Mairet goes on to speak of "the personal quality, which had an enormous effect upon others; a kind of completely unassumed and unassuming dignity, which was a power; the power of a person who, however friendly and gracious he may be, as Tom Eliot certainly was, is dedicated to something beyond and above us—and himself".

Let him have the last word—the word of a Christian believer and a churchman. It is one of his images of the Atonement, the image of Christ the healer, from *East Coker*:

"The wounded surgeon plies the steel
That questions the distempered part;
Beneath the bleeding hands we feel
The sharp compassion of the healer's art
Resolving the enigma of the fever chart",

with (as Miss Sayers points out) the other images: the Church as "the dying nurse"; the world as "our hospital" endowed by Adam "the ruined Millionaire". As we bid farewell to Thomas Stearns Eliot and commend him to that eternal realm, of which he had so many wistful and tantalising glimpses, to the care of God the Lord of all life, let us recall two of his utterances appropriate to the solemn occasion of his departure.

From *The Waste Land*:

"What have we given?
My friend, blood shaking my heart
The awful daring of a moment's surrender
Which an age of prudence can never retract
By this, and this only, we have existed
Which is not to be found in our obituaries".

Last of all from *Little Gidding*:

"What the dead had no speech for, when living,
They can tell you, being dead: the communication
Of the dead is tongued with fire beyond the language of the living".

He who blessed us by his presence is now surely blessed by the fulfilment of that truth in himself. May light perpetual shine upon him.

28. Cuthbert Aikman Simpson, D.D., Dean of Christ Church, 1959–1969

"The zeal of thy House has consumed me".
(Psalm lxix.9)

THOSE of you who worship here regularly will feel desolate at seeing the Dean's stall empty, for he was hardly ever absent from it. His sudden death in sleep last Sunday night lays a heavy weight of sorrow upon this College and Cathedral, and upon all in this University and outside, who knew his forceful and friendly presence. But in this sorrow, for one thing we are thankful: he passed out of this life without irksome illness or pain, and, until the day before, in full possession of his powers.

Others of you who may be attending our Cathedral only this once will please forgive us for treating this service as a domestic occasion.

Cuthbert Aikman Simpson arrived here in 1954 from across the Atlantic to become Regius Professor of Hebrew and Canon of Christ Church. He had been here before as a Rhodes scholar undergraduate soon after the first world war. After four years as Professor and Canon he was appointed Dean. Strangers present today should know that a Dean of Christ Church presides over both the College as a place of learning and teaching and also over the Cathedral body of Canons and other ministers. I was already here when Dr. Simpson came, preceded by his wife Jessie—the sweetest lady you could meet—whose death eight years ago was a dreadful personal calamity for him.

I could tell on his arrival what a deep satisfaction he found in teaching his own chosen subject of Old Testament religion and theology as an essential background for Christian belief, in his old University and College. When he became Dean his administrative tasks meant some abatement of his scholarly pursuits. But it brought out of him in excellence one of the three qualities our Lord Jesus Christ expected of his disciples—the quality of zeal—the other two of Christ's requirements being Faith and Repentance.

To my mind, zeal in the handling of College and Cathedral affairs was Cuthbert Simpson's outstanding characteristic. He loved this place and enjoyed almost every minute in the tenure of his office. That does not overlook the occasional growl over such things as an indecisive protracted discussion, or a hitch in procedure, or resistance to his deeply felt wishes. It was his zeal that carried through several notable transformations in the ten years of his Deanery: first of all enlarging the housing capacity of the college by new buildings, appealing to friends and old members and getting response from them. This same energy secured a special gallery to house and display our valued collection of pictures. He hoped he would live to see these buildings completed, and he was rewarded.

It was out of his zeal that fellowship was fostered with the young, undergraduates, junior teachers and choristers, as well as with more sedate and permanent members of the Christ Church organisation. Under his initiative the society known as Friends of the Cathedral, which had been started by Dr. Lowe, his predecessor, grew into an influential body of people sustaining the Cathedral and meeting many of its needs.

By his zeal this Cathedral was cleaned, embellished and enriched with exquisite furnishings; and our contacts with diocese and city were enlarged; the services and music were given an added dignity and splendour. The singing and the choir were a special delight and the object of great care to him. But these were only the outward signs of Dr. Simpson's devotion; behind all that went on in public lay his regular presence at the daily offices of morning and evening prayer: those in the morning at seven-thirty, at which only chapter colleagues and a few faithful joined in. This cathedral and its worship was for him a kind of spiritual fountain of refreshment, which enabled him to carry the multifarious and exacting tasks, which his position laid upon him.

A man is known by the things he likes doing off duty. The Dean was particularly concerned to interpret the message of the Bible to people of today. Those who listened to his sermons from this pulpit will have noticed that he embarked on his subject with a transatlantic directness without any timid speculation about how much Jones would swallow. He spent hours devising improved selections for the lessons read in church. "Your Dean", someone said to me, "has got a thing about Lectionaries". Indeed, he had a concern that the scriptures should become a lively oracle for this age and generation. He had an ingenious interest in the Genesis stories of Creation; also in the civic life of the Hebrew people pictured in the Book of Judges. He wrote a book years ago about Jeremiah, called *Jeremiah, Prophet of My People*. He there corrected the popular idea of Jeremiah as a complaining pessimist. That prophet's appeal to him was rather that in the severest trial Israel had to endure, in her faithlessness and exile, Jeremiah knew what had to be given up, because he knew what must be kept and preserved. Simpson responded to a preacher who had to endure the taunt that his religious message was in conflict with the false cocksure patriotism of a wayward people.

The Dean's preaching message was often fortified by some pieces of modern religious literature. More than once he borrowed my copy of Dorothy Sayers' drama *The Zeal of Thy House* and I was interested in the fascination it had for him.

The play is woven round the actual figure of a Norman architect, William of Sens, who rebuilt much of Canterbury Cathedral in the twelfth century, having been hesitatingly chosen by the chapter to reconstruct the burnt-out choir. I lay no significance upon the fact that the monks of that time showed some nervousness about their prior's decision in the appointment! It was rather two religious themes that appealed to Simpson. First, the awful picture of God's judgment upon the architect for an arrogance, which set his superb craftsmanship defiantly over against the weightier matters of the divine law. William is crippled by an accident when the rope holding his cradle to the roof gives way at a weak point. Two of the brethren had been told beforehand to test the rope by running it through their fingers. Distracted by their curiosity in what might be a fine newspaper scandal about the architect and a lady, they let the flaw pass without noticing it. The other side of that terrible lapse is the vision of Michael the Archangel up aloft, cutting through, with his sword of judgment, the rope at the very spot where it snapped. It was this perceptive handling by Miss Sayers, in the play, of the union between man's free action and the overarching purpose of God, that struck a chord in Dr. Simpson's mind. This problem of the identity of human freedom and God's providence is one, which no human mind has ever resoled by discursive thought. But it can be conveyed by the poet and the dramatist. I guess that the title *Zeal of Thy House* touched his heart because of his own zeal for this particular house of God.

Besides his studies and his favourite literature a man is known by other things. One is his attitude to possessions. Doctor Simpson, though not a very rich man, had considerable private means, and his use of it was a matter of conscience and method. He regarded money as something requiring the exercise of stewardship. Much that he bestowed secretly is known only to recipients. So far as he could help it he did not do his alms to be seen of men. But much of his generosity could not be hidden: his magnanimous hospitality; his support of causes he believed in; his gifts of things to adorn this church; and God knows in how many other ways. He was for sure one of the few fairly rich men who will get through the needle's eye.

A man is also known through the people he lives and works closely with from day to day. Among these, I would like publicly to pay tribute to four people who were devoted to him. Mr. and Mrs. Stockford who kept his house and cared for his well-being; the Revd. Michael Watts, our Cathedral chaplain and sacrist; Miss Celia Clissold, the Dean's secretary. These two, bearing the weight of sudden grief last Monday morning, courageously conveyed their feelings into a masterly managing of arrangements for the last rites of yesterday.

Lastly, a man is known by his temperament. Cuthbert Simpson had a temperament, which called out people's affections. He wore his heart on his sleeve. When his emotions were involved he could give way to tears, and like Winston Churchill he was not ashamed. He could also be peppery, and those who caught it might smart for a minute, but then the humorous and benign light of his eyes would dispel the hurt. "Our new Dean is a very quick tempered man" said the head verger when Dr. Simpson first came to the Deanery, "but it doesn't last; it's like milk boiling over". One of the human things about him was his enjoyment of a point against himself. He repeated with glee a description made of him, in view of the relatively late age, at which he became Dean, by someone who joined up two incongruous scripture phrases: "He goeth about like a roaring lion, because he knoweth he hath but a short time". "Roaring", however, is not quite the right word for those impetuous little explosions, which we tolerated and loved him for, even when they were sometimes too audible in church.

In his last speech, at the College gaudy less than a week ago, with prominent people and old members present, he spoke movingly about what Christ Church had meant to him in his undergraduate days. His affectionate nature was infectious; so were his enthusiasms, though sometimes hard to keep up with.

For us in Christ Church his was a very dynamic presence. The dynamo has stopped, but light from the accumulator, which he charged up in the last ten years, will shine brightly for a very long time—and he will be watching for the sparks.

God rest his soul. Amen.

Afterword

CANON Vigo Auguste Demant's professional academic career was connected with the Christ Church College at the University of Oxford, where he was Regius Professor of Moral and Pastoral Theology for over 20 years. It was in 1925 that the Regius Chair of Pastoral Theology in Christ Church was renamed as the Regius Chair of Moral and Pastoral Theology. Its reputation continued to grow and has become the leading academic centre of Anglican moral theology or Christian ethics. Robert Lawrence Ottley was the first Regius Professor of Moral and Pastoral Theology at Christ Church, having been first Regius Chair of Pastoral Theology to which he was appointed in 1903. He was succeeded by Kenneth Escott Kirk in 1933, who continued as Regius Professor and Canon of Christ Church until 1938, a year after he became Bishop of Oxford. Then, Leonard Hodgson held the chair till 1944 and Robert Cecil Mortimer followed. Mortimer resigned from the Chair upon his appointment as Bishop of Exeter and was succeeded by Vigo Auguste Demant in 1949, who continued as Regius Professor of Moral and Pastoral Theology as well as Canon of Christ Church until his retirement in 1971. His successor for eight years was Peter Baelz. In 1982 Oliver O'Donovan was appointed Regius Professor and Canon of Christ Church, a position he carried on till 2006. Currently the Regius Chair is held by Nigel Biggar.

Vigo Auguste Demant was born in Newcastle-upon-Tyne on 8 November 1893 of mixed origin—his father was Thorvald Conrad Frederick Demant, a Unitarian and professional teacher of modern languages of Huguenot descent, a follower of Auguste Comte and his Danish mother was Emilie Thora Wildemann[1]. After spending some time in his hometown, he continued to

---

[1]   V.A. Demant's biographical data presented here draw on several sources: Demant's biographies from the *Oxford Dictionary of National Biography* by A. Cunningham and

attend school in France and even studied briefly at the Sorbonne. Upon his return to England he carried on his studies and in 1913 received a diploma in engineering from Armstrong College (which later became a part of Newcastle University). Then in 1916 Demant moved to Oxford to study anthropology at Exeter and Manchester Colleges and to prepare for Unitarian ministry. Between 1917 and 1919 he ministered to the Unitarian congregation at Newbury. Having met Bishop of Oxford Charles Gore and being influenced by him, he converted and was received into the Church of England by Gore himself and affiliated himself with its High Church tradition that preserved close links with continental Catholicism. It was in this context that he met and was influenced by such Christian European intellectuals as J. Maritain or N. Berdyaev. In 1920 Demant was ordained an Anglican priest and ministered first in two parishes in Oxford—St. Thomas's and St. Michael's and then at St. Nicholas' mission in Plumstead, Norfolk. After three curacies in London in 1933 he became Vicar of St. John the Divine in Richmond, Surrey and in 1942 was appointed Canon and Chancellor of St. Paul's Cathedral in London. Finally, seven years later he became Canon of Christ Church, which is attached to the Regius Professorship of Moral and Pastoral Theology at the University of Oxford. In 1925 he married Marjorie Tickner and they had three children—a son and two daughters. Vigo Auguste Demant died on 3 March 1983.

From his early years Demant's scholarly and pastoral interests focused on sociological issues, which he always attempted to see and address in light of Catholic theology. It was his encounter in 1926 and long collaboration thereafter with Maurice Bennington Reckitt, an influential layman and author, as presented by A. Louth in *Foreword*, that made a lasting impact on Vigo Demant shaping his entire priestly and academic career. Reckitt and Demant, joined, among others, by W.G. Peck and P.E.T. Widdrington, J.H. Oldham, R.H. Tawney, T.S. Eliot, formed Christendom Group and developed Christian sociology. In their Christian analysis of society, rooted particularly in incarnational theology, they meant an "application of Christian moral and ethical teaching to the social problems of the day" (R. Jeffery). V.A. Demant was the leading intellectual in that circle. In order to promote their ideas they established a quarterly called "Christendom: A Journal of Christian Sociology" in 1931 whose last (80th) issue appeared in December 1950. Beside Demant,

---

from the *Dictionary of Historical Theology* by I. Markham, the article *V.A. Demant* by A. Louth, *Speech of Presentation* (at the University of Durham) by W.B. Fisher, Demant's obituary from "The Times" as well as some private notes prepared for me by R. Jeffery

Reckitt and their closest collaborators already mentioned, among its authors were also: Ch. Dawson, E.L. Mascall, K.E. Kirk, N. Berdyaev (Berdiaeff), J. Maritain, Ch. Smyth, D.G. Peck, A.M. Ramsey, T.S. Eliot, F.L. Cross, P. McLaughlin, J.V. Langmead Casserley, H. Slesser, A.R. Vidler, Ch. Williams, D.M. MacKinnon, D. Munby, H.A. Hodges, Ph. Mairet, H.A.T. Bennet, C.E. Hudson, J.F. Fletcher.

Demant gradually became a very influential figure in the Church of England. Being able to read in several languages his expertise covered theology, philosophy, sociology, anthropology and economics. It is thus right to say that he "produced a coherent theology, which carried forward an Anglican Catholic tradition of social thought" (A. Cunningham). In recognition of his "intellectual and moral eminence" (W.B. Fisher) he was made Doctor Litterarum in theology by the University of Oxford in 1940 and in 1974 he received an honorary Doctor Divinitatis of the University of Durham.

The Christendom Group's Christian sociology continued to develop after the Second World War, particularly in the Anglo-Catholic Summer Schools of Sociology (or Church Union Summer Schools of Sociology). Though all members of the Group had their own contributions to this project, it was Vigo Demant who was known as its "thinker" (I. Markham). Still before the war Demant worked for the Church of England's Christian Social Council, which was one of the major effects of the 1924 Conference on Christian Politics, Economics and Citizenship (COPEC). As research director for the Council he either wrote or edited and published several books as reports: *The Miners' Distress and the Coal Problem: An Outline for Christian Thought and Action* (London: SCM Press 1929), *The Just Price: An Outline of the Medieval Doctrine and an Examination of Its Possible Equivalent To-day* (London: SCM Press 1930), *This Unemployment: Disaster or Opportunity?* (London: SCM Press 1931). Similar problems were dealt with in the book he had edited earlier: *Coal: A Challenge to the National Conscience* (London: Hogarth Press 1927). Among his smaller publications were: *How to Prevent the Next War* (London: Stanhope Press 1937), *The Responsibility and Scope of Pastoral Theology To-day* (Oxford: Clarendon Press 1950). Demant's major books are the following: *God, Man and Society: An Introduction to Christian Sociology* (London: SCM Press 1933), *Christian Polity* (London: Faber and Faber 1936), *The Religious Prospect* (London: F. Muller 1939), *Theology of Society: More Essays in Christian Polity* (London: Faber and Faber 1947), *What Is Happening to Us?* (London: Dacre Press 1951), *Religion and the Decline of Capitalism* (London: Faber and Faber 1952), *A Two-Way Religion: Talks on the Inner and Outer Life* (London: Mowbray

1957), *An Exposition of Christian Sexual Ethics* (London: Hodder and Stoughton 1963), *The Idea of a Natural Order with an Essay on Modern Asceticism* (Philadelphia: Fortress Press 1966). He also edited *Faith that Illuminates* (London: The Centenary Press 1935) and *Our Culture: Its Christian Roots and Present Crisis* (London: SPCK 1947).

Vigo A. Demant was deeply concerned with various social and pastoral issues of European (not only English) society and civilization. Many of his observations, though made decades ago and in a different context, have not lost in significance. Notwithstanding, it is probably right to state that at the heart of his concern was the Christian heart of culture. This was very much in line with the well-known conviction of T.S. Eliot: "It is in Christianity that our arts have developed; it is in Christianity that the laws of Europe have—until recently—been rooted. It is against a background of Christianity that all our thought has significance. An individual European may not believe that the Christian Faith is true, and yet what he says, and makes, and does, will all spring out of his heritage of Christian culture and depend on that culture for its meaning". Canon Demant believed that human life, whether individual or social in all its aspects, was in need of the spiritual, in fact of God Himself. The obvious reason for that is that the human being, though a "natural animal", is "essentially a spiritual being" and as such is "dependent both upon natural things and processes and upon the Divine source of his spiritual life". Thus it is right to say that Demant's primary focus was on the human being (the human person) in all his or her nature and both earthly and eternal vocation. Nevertheless, Demant's concern in this aspect was not so much anthropocentric as theocentric or Christocentric because what he had in mind was the Christian doctrine of man. He believed it was only in the light of God, who made Himself "manifest in Jesus the Christ, God the Son, the divine principle of creation and redemption", that every man and woman can find their meaning, which transcends earthly life. The basic truth is that "God is the ground of our existence" and so one cannot ignore the "connection between the Creator and the Creation". As he put it in one of his sermons published here, just as "the world's meaning cannot be found inside the world itself" in the same way man needs to reach beyond this world to the Creator God and to see oneself as a "participator in the divine action". In his frequent writings on modern civilization Demant would similarly point to a "spiritual urge, an insatiability in man, which demands something more than self-preservation or happiness or security". This made Demant believe in what may be labelled an ecclesial dimension of man's life since it was the Church's mission to "meet the hunger" of humanity with "the true bread of eternal life, which is the status of man she exists to proclaim and to minister". In this sense the defence of the spiritual could be emphasized as Demant's continuous effort to achieve what he called a "true humanism".

Thus, though a sociologist engaged in all sorts of social problems in many ways, as his publications and practical activities prove, he remained a theologian who sought to understand the world and man in it from a Christian or Divine perspective. While one can and should rightly search for all actual reasons for what makes life on earth unjust, painful or even inhuman, Demant always had in mind that, theologically speaking, the origin of all evils was the Fall. Hence, both the world and man in all aspects of his life are in need of Redemption. This Redemption, which is "always a restoration", can and has indeed come from God, the "source and end of the created world". Christianity, being a gospel, continues to proclaim that it is God who restores "things to their true nature". It is His Son Jesus Christ, the Redeemer, who "purifies and transforms the creation".

While some would call it a coincidence, I believe (again, a Christian perspective...) my own meeting with Prof. Andrew Louth in Oxford quite a time ago was providential. My earlier research in V.A. Demant's writings (including his unpublished Gifford Lectures notes, to which I found my way through the late Adrianne Demant, Canon Demant's daughter-in-law) made me think he was that kind of man and scholar who deserved a new attention and would make valuable and useful reading years later. I am genuinely grateful to Fr. Louth for his confidence as well as for his assistance in the preparation of this "miscellany of preachments" for publication. The reader of this book should also know that its title is a quotation from the apocryphal Second Book of Esdras, and Canon Demant intended its phrasing as in the original.

Sławomir Nowosad

Index of Names